Officially Withdrawn

POLITICS AND HIGHER EDUCATION

POLITICS
AND
HIGHER EDUCATION

John D. Millett

The University of Alabama Press
University, Alabama

Contents

Preface

When Dr. Coleman R. Ransone, Jr., invited me to present five lectures under the auspices of the Southern Regional Training program in Public Administration, I was delighted to be able to accept the invitation. Since my retirement as chancellor of the Ohio Board of Regents in the summer of 1972, I had wanted to find time to put in writing some of my recollections of the nineteen years spent as president of a state university and as chancellor of the public higher education system in Ohio. The invitation to present these lectures ended my procrastination and compelled me to get busy at this writing chore.

A second reason for my interest in writing these recollections is my long-standing conviction that students of political science and students of public administration have too long ignored the whole field of higher education. The administration of a state university and the administration of a state board of higher education are experiences in public administration. It is remarkable how so many persons professing an interest in politics and administration have somehow tended to avoid any realistic view of higher education. I would like to help fill that gap.

There is a third reason why I have been willing to present these recollections while they are still very fresh in my memory. Administration is a very personal business. It is easy to talk about models and images of the college or university president, and one of these days we shall no doubt talk about the models and images of the state government higher education administrator. Yet the generalizations by no means convey the richness of individual administrative styles, personal inclinations and attitudes, and personality characteristics. Only the case study can begin to offer the full sense of individual endeavor.

These lectures are not an autobiography. Nor are they an apologia. I have not wanted to indulge in any criticisms of persons or in any recriminations about motivations. Many anecdotes have been omitted because I wanted to present broad issues rather than trivial conflicts. And yet, this record is personal, and no doubt suffers the defects of just such an account.

Among our fifty states, the traditions and structure of public higher education are quite different. I believe that there is no typical state government and no representative state system of higher education. Although some scholars today pursue their research by a sampling of state experience, I doubt very much that this practice is an adequate basis for generalization of experience and trends. Certainly, I do not present this account as anything more than a case study representing the point of view of a participant-observer in the higher education politics of one single state. I am quite sure that other persons in other states have had quite different experiences.

In one particular respect my own experience is quite unique among those individuals who have served in recent years as state higher education executive officers. I had been president of a state university in Ohio for eleven years before I became chancellor for the Ohio Board of Regents. Among executive officers of state planning and coordinating boards, I have not known any other person who had had experience as a state university president prior to assuming the state government role. When state governments create a single state-wide governing board, it is not unusual for the chief executive officer to have been a state university president.

In any event, my experience of eight years in a state capital followed upon eleven years in a state university. I think this sequence made a great deal of difference in my behavior. When I became chancellor, I was the senior state university president in terms of years of service, except for the president of Central State College, who was at retirement age. I had been through eleven years of struggle on the state government scene. In large part, I saw my state government role to be that of accomplishing objectives that had been formulated in these earlier years.

Moreover, I was not disposed to consider my role as inferior to or subservient to the other state university presidents. I am sure this attitude was little appreciated by the state university presidents. After all, the prestige status in American higher education attaches to the position of college or university president. It does not attach in any like degree to the position of state higher education executive officer. Moreover, I suspect that in most instances state university presidents prefer that a nonpresident occupy these state government positions.

I offer these comments only to emphasize the uniqueness of the experience related in these lectures. It is from all experiences of this kind in all fifty states that we must draw such generalizations as are appropriate about the structure and operation of public higher education in the United States.

I would like to think that my background in political science and in public administration had something to do with my understanding and my performance of the role of state university president and state government chancellor. I considered this background as important and useful preparation for the tasks I assumed. In addition, my five years of government service in Washington from 1941 to 1946 provided useful experience and observation. In those years, I was a staff officer rather than an administrator, first in the Executive Office of the President and then in one of the three commands of the War Department. There is a good deal of difference between being a staff officer and a commanding officer, but I am sure the first kind of position is a necessary preparation for the second.

I think what I acquired above all else from my prewar and wartime experience in Washington was a sense of the urgency of administrative action. My commanding general in the Pentagon had a slogan hanging on the wall in his office that read: "Any reasonable action today is preferable to a search for the ideal action tomorrow." I never have forgotten those words.

Washington, D.C.   JOHN D. MILLETT
February, 1974

POLITICS AND HIGHER EDUCATION

1

State Universities and State Government:
The Miami Years 1953–1964

FOR ELEVEN YEARS DURING THE PERIOD FROM 1953 TO 1964, I
served as president of Miami University, one of the state
universities of Ohio. It is not my intention here, however, to
indulge in autobiographical detail about the experience of
those years insofar as the university itself is concerned. A
state university president has an internal and an external
role to fulfill. Internally, he is concerned with the leadership of a unique organizational structure of various con-
stituencies. Externally, he is concerned with the relationships of a state university to other state universities, to the
agencies and organs of decision-making of state government, and to the various publics that determine the popular
image of a state university.

In this chapter, I want to explore more particularly one
part of these external relationships: the relationships with
state government. In other words, I am concerned with the
politics of higher education. I must hasten to add, however,
that this exploration is necessarily quite personal. I shall
recount experiences and observations that arose in connection with my particular role as president of Miami University. I do not wish to suggest that these experiences and
observations were necessarily representative of experiences
and observations that other persons in other states would
recount. I do have some reason to believe that with appropriate modifications for differences in personalities and
situations, this telling is not without some utility for others.

I think it may be useful in this context, however, for me to sketch very briefly something about the history of Miami University and something about the history of higher education in Ohio and in the United States. This information may be useful in providing a background for the matters that I wish to consider in this chapter. Such a background must be sketched in very broad strokes, and must omit much in illustrative detail.

Miami University was founded by an act of the General Assembly of Ohio, which became law on February 17, 1809. This legislation came about in response to the admonition contained in the Northwest Ordinance of 1787 that "schools and the means to education shall be forever encouraged." This exhortation found practical expression in subsequent legislation of the federal Congress confirming a purchase of land by John Cleves Symmes of New Jersey in the Ohio territory north of the Ohio River and lying between the Little Miami and the Great Miami rivers. The federal legislation approved by President George Washington on May 2, 1792, directed Symmes to set aside "one complete township or tract of land, of six mile square" to be granted and held in trust for the sole and exclusive intent and purpose of erecting and establishing therein an academy and other public schools and seminaries of learning, and endowing and supporting the same.

John Cleves Symmes obtained a land grant of one million acres from the Congress of the United States, land that stretched from what is today the City of Cincinnati almost all the way to Dayton. But in the 1790s it was largely a wilderness, and when Ohio became a state in 1803, the western part of the state was still only sparsely settled. On February 17, 1809, the General Assembly of Ohio enacted a law establishing the Miami University and endowing it in perpetuity with the township of land which the federal law of 1792 had directed to be set aside. Only then was it discovered that in his sale of land Symmes had forgotten to reserve one complete township to support a seminary of learning. Prodded by the political leaders of the newly created state, Symmes bought a township of land west of the Great Miami River on the westernmost border of Ohio.

Eventually, in 1824, Miami University opened its doors in the village of Oxford, situated on a ridge in the middle of its thirty-six sections of land grant, and began the instruction of students in that classical curriculum which was the basis of American higher learning in the first half of the Nineteenth Century. In the early 1840s, Miami University was a flourishing college, with the fourth largest enrollment in the entire United States. An early "understanding" among Ohio political leaders had determined that Ohio University, founded in 1804, would be under Methodist influence and Miami University under Presbyterian influence. Doctrinal disputes within the Presbyterian church decimated the Miami faculty and student body and led to the creation of a strictly Presbyterian controlled college, the College of Wooster.

Other difficulties also beset Miami. The third president, resigning in 1849, set forth several "causes of evil" that he said the university had suffered in recent years. The first of these causes of evil, he declared, was a prevalent misconception of the true and proper object for which a college is established. In particular, President MacMaster attacked the idea that a college should communicate the special knowledge and skills by which men are fitted for the ordinary manual and industrial occupations of life. The second cause of evil from which the University suffered was the "inordinate devotion of the great mass of the community to mere material objects" and the consequent limited desire for a liberal education. In the third place, MacMaster criticized the failure of persons to understand that the proper preparation for professional studies was an "exact and sound scholarship" in "disciplinary training." Please observe that I am quoting from an *1849* document. And the

fourth cause of evil for the University was the establishment
of numerous church colleges. There were in 1849, President MacMaster asserted, no fewer than thirteen such
church colleges in Ohio belonging to particular religious
denominations and drawing into them students who
otherwise might have gone elsewhere, meaning Miami
University. There follows in President MacMaster's address
a fascinating contrast of the relative merits of higher education under Church auspices and those of the State. And the
fifth cause of past difficulties, MacMaster declared, arose
from an "officious and very mischievous intermeddling
from without in the internal affairs of the institution." And
here follows an equally illuminating discussion on the
merits of university autonomy. The President attacked
politicians, newspapers, and church leaders for interfering
with the University.

But Miami University survived the vicissitudes of the
1850s and the tragedy of Civil War only to succumb to
financial disaster in 1873. In the fifty years from 1824 to
1873 Miami drew its income from two primary sources:
land rents from the township and student fees. But the
General Assembly of Ohio saw fit in the 1840s to freeze the
level of land rents, and, beset by small enrollments and
postwar inflation, Miami University closed its doors in
1873. I once had occasion to go back over the names and
careers of the 1000 graduates of Miami University between
1824 and 1873 and I found that one-third had become
ministers, one-third had become lawyers, and the remaining one-third had entered many different occupations
from medicine and business to journalism, teaching, and
farming. Among those graduates were some twenty-three
persons whose careers are recorded in the *Dictionary of
American Biography* including one President of the United
States, Benjamin Harrison; two governors of Ohio, William
Dennison and Andrew Harris; a famous Chicago preacher,
David Swing; a president of both the University of

Pittsburgh and New York University, Henry Mitchell Mac-
Cracken; the inventor of ticker tape and then president of
the University of Missouri, Samuel Spahr Laws; the founder of the New York Public Library, John Shaw Billings; the
great New York journalist and publisher, Whitelaw Reid;
the founder of the New York law firm of Sullivan and
Cromwell, Algernon Sidney Sullivan; and the railroad and
mining engineer who was first to survey the Colorado River
including the Grand Canyon, Robert B. Stanton.

There were others who attended Miami University but
obtained their degrees elsewhere: men like Oliver P. Mor-
ton, the Civil War governor of Indiana; Admiral Stephen
C. Rowan of the United States Navy; James Carter Beard,
distinguished artist and illustrator; William McMurtie, industrial chemist and founder of the Royal Baking Powder
Company; and John Henry Patterson, founder of the National Cash Register Company.

Miami University reopened its doors in 1885, when the
State of Ohio decided that it would have to provide both
capital improvement appropriations and current operating
appropriations for the three institutions of higher education in Ohio that were sponsored by the State: Ohio University, Miami University, and the newly established Ohio State
University, which had been created in 1870 as the
beneficiary of the federal Morrill Land Grant Act of 1862.
From 1885 onward the "new" Miami was in every sense a
state university. In 1902 the General Assembly directed
Ohio University and Miami University to create normal
schools, and then in 1906 the General Assembly wrestled
with the issue of the respective missions to be assigned the
three universities. In 1910 the General Assembly directed
the establishment of two new teachers colleges, which in the
1930s became Bowling Green State University and Kent
State University. In 1951 a sixth state institution was
created, Central State College, a college composed predom-
inantly of black students and a spin-off from a private

church-related college sponsored by the African Methodist Episcopal Church, Wilberforce University.

When I came from Columbia University to Miami University as its sixteenth president on July 1, 1953, the University had its fair share of accumulated problems. I suspect these difficulties were neither greater nor less than those experienced by most state universities in the first half of the Twentieth Century. Miami had developed three professional schools besides its College of Arts and Science: a School of Education, a School of Business Administration, and a School of Fine Arts. The graduate program was small and oriented toward school teachers. The enrollment had grown from around 600 students in 1910, to 1500 students in 1920, to 2000 students in 1930, to 3000 students in 1940. Immediately after the end of World War II, the enrollment jumped to 4600 students and reached a peak of 5400 students in 1948. Enrollment dropped back to 5000 students in 1952 and returned to 5100 students the year I arrived.

Neither capital improvements nor current operating support had kept pace with enrollment. The State of Ohio had never been overly generous with its state-supported universities. During the depression years, capital improvement appropriations had ceased, and only the introduction of a sales tax in 1935 had saved the state from bankruptcy. Ohio was not to get a state income tax until 1971. Moreover, the State had made no effort to obtain public works grants from the federal government after 1933. The only evidence I could find of PWA projects on the Miami campus in 1953 was two rebuilt residence halls for which the University, not the State of Ohio, had contributed the required matching funds. The great increase of students after 1945 had been housed in barracks brought from Army posts as war surplus property, and some instruction had been provided in the same kind of structures.

During the war years when state governments had been encouraged to maintain existing tax levels while curtailing state activity, the State of Ohio had accumulated a surplus. This surplus had built two new classroom buildings completed in 1951 and 1952, along with a Navy ROTC armory. But these facilities had done no more than compensate for the deficiency in space accumulated during the long drought in construction during the 1930s. In this same ten years, enrollment had increased by about 50 percent. Moreover, the Miami University academic plant in 1953 included one building the major parts of which were 100 years old or more, and three classroom buildings plus a women's gymnasium which were over forty years of age. All of these buildings were in need of replacement or major renovation.

When I turned to the current operating budget in 1953, I was also perturbed by what I found. My first concern was that the University lacked a budget system and a comprehensive statement of income and expenditure for approval by the Board of Trustees. My second concern was the relatively modest rate of instructional expenditures. The average faculty salary in 1952–53 had been around $4700 for a nine-month academic year. The average salary of a full professor was slightly more than $6000 a year. The student-faculty ratio in 1952–53 was nineteen to one. The total instructional budget, as I was able to reconstruct it, came to around $530 per student. Of this cost, the State of Ohio provided about $400 per student; the remainder was obtained primarily from charges to students.

I think it may be appropriate to pause here for a moment to say something about the role of a state university president as I perceived it in 1953. For the previous eight years, I had been an associate professor and professor of government in the graduate faculty of the social sciences at Columbia University in New York. As a faculty member I had never seen a budget or a financial report for Columbia. The faculty task was to worry about instruction and scholarship. The administrators had the job of worrying about the University as a university. I did not know the salaries of my colleagues in my own department until the semester when I served as acting executive officer of the department. For three years, however, between 1949 and 1952, I had served as executive director of the Commission on Financing Higher Education, a private group of presidents and trustees sponsored by the Association of American Universities and financed by the Rockefeller Foundation and the Carnegie Corporation of New York. My impressions about the role of the college or university president had been drawn from this experience.

It was clear to me that as of 1953 the college or university president was only to a limited extent an educational leader. Essentially, the role was that of an institutional leader, preoccupied with the status of the college or university as an institution, with the social expectations about the institution, and with the income and expense of the institution. I had no illusions in 1953 about the demands to be made upon the president of Miami University. Unlike some others I knew, I was prepared to operate within the constraints imposed by the unique characteristics of the academic environment.

The Inter-University Council of Ohio

I became acquainted with the existence of an Inter-University Council of the five state universities and the one state college when I visited The Ohio State University in October, 1950. As a part of my study of financing higher education under the auspices of the Association of American Universities, I undertook in 1950–51 to visit a substantial number of colleges and universities throughout the United States. During the course of a day's conversation with President Howard L. Bevis of Ohio State, he recounted the origins and the operation of this somewhat unique experience in inter-institutional cooperation among the state-supported higher education institutions of Ohio. Not by the furthest stretch of the imagination did it occur to me that three years later I would be a participant in this Council.

In 1934 Martin L. Davey, Democrat of Kent, was elected as the Governor of Ohio. Soon after his inauguration in January, 1935, the Governor helped to accomplish legislation that changed the designations of Kent and Bowling Green State Colleges to Kent and Bowling Green State Universities. In several other ways the Governor indicated his disposition to advance the interests of the state university located in his home community. As a consequence, the presidents of Miami University and of The Ohio State University in 1938 took the leadership in organizing a mutual protective association on behalf of all five state universities. The presidents and trustees of Ohio University, Bowling Green State University, and Kent State University decided that it was in their long-range self interest to join in the creation and functioning of this Inter-University Council of Ohio. The Inter-University Council then came into being in 1939.

The Inter-University Council included two representatives from each state university: the president and a member of the board of trustees. In addition, the chief fiscal officer of each institution regularly attended all meetings of the Council and played a prominent part in all discussions. The five state universities committed themselves to three obligations: first, to recognize the exclusive mission of Ohio State to award the doctor's degree in graduate study; second, to present to the chief executive and the General Assembly a commonly agreed-upon statement of the current operating and capital appropriation needs of all five institutions and to defend these in concert one with another; and to cooperate in all matters of legislation and other public interests concerning the state universities. In practice, the Inter-University Council was primarily active in two areas of common concern: the presentation of state appropriation requests for current operations and the presentation of capital improvement appropriation requests.

When the Inter-University Council came into existence in 1939 for the mutual protection of the state universities in their relation to state government, Governor Davey had been defeated in the 1938 general election in his bid for a third two-year term by John W. Bricker, Republican of Columbus. Inaugurated in January, 1939, Governor Bricker served three terms, until January, 1945. A graduate of Ohio State, Governor Bricker was generally disposed to be friendly toward all the state universities, provided it didn't cost too much. If the state universities wished to get together in determining the distribution of the state appropriation available to them, Governor Bricker was agreeable to the arrangement. So was Governor Frank J. Lausche, Democrat of Cleveland, who served from 1945 to 1947 and again from 1949 to 1957.

The method of procedure described to me in 1950 by President Bevis was the method of procedure with which I became familiar after 1953 as a member of the Inter-University Council. I should add that in 1948, Wilberforce University as a state-aided institution was added to the Council membership, and when Central State College was created by law in 1951 as a separate full-fledged state institution of higher education split off from Wilberforce University, it became a member of the Council. The practice was something as follows:

In the autumn of an even-numbered year at the time when the Governor was preparing his biennial budget recommendations to be given to the General Assembly early in the next year, the Inter-University Council would be convened by its chairman, who was one of the state university presidents. The chairmanship was held for a one-year term by the president of one of the six state institutions in the alphabetical order of the name of the institution. A president was not eligible to serve as chairman, however, until he had been a president for at least two years. When thus convened, the members of the Council discussed their respective needs and the prospects for obtaining more appropriations in the next biennium than had been received in the current biennium. After this discussion and general agreement about a total appropriation amount to request for all six institutions, the chairman was delegated to begin negotiations on behalf of all institutions with the Governor's office. The Governor's representative in these discussions was the State Director of Finance who served as the Governor's budget officer. These negotiations might continue over a period of several weeks, the chairman of the Council insisting that the state universities needed an increased appropriation and the Director of Finance insisting that state revenues were limited and that any increase in the appropriation would be very difficult to obtain. Once or twice during these negotiations the chairman might call the Inter-University Council together to report his impressions of progress in the negotiations and to ask for advice and ammunition to employ in the final stages of discussion with the Director of Finance.

Eventually the chairman, usually in December, would call the Council members together to report the final amount of the total higher education appropriation acceptable to the Director of Finance and the Governor. I cannot recall at any time in eleven years that the Governor actually took a direct hand in these appropriation negotiations. It was understood that the Director of Finance spoke for the Governor and that any attempt to go over the head of the Director of Finance directly to the Governor would be a waste of time and an extremely unwise effort. Once the appropriation total for all the state universities had been set, the Inter-University Council began its real chore of arriving at a distribution of the total among the six institutions. This effort was likely to spread over two or three meetings, although there was inevitably a time limit when budget details had to be reported to the Director of Finance. In this distribution, the only way in which the Council could agree upon the fair share for each institution was to make the distribution correspond more or less to enrollment. It was recognized that Ohio State should receive something more than its proportion of total enrollment because of its graduate work at the doctoral level and because of its medical school. It was also recognized that Central State should receive something more than its proportion of total enrollment because of its small size. With about 49 percent of total enrollment, Ohio State usually received about 55 percent of the distribution. With just 2 percent of total enrollment, Central State would usually receive 4 or 5 percent of the total. Thus Bowling Green, Miami, Kent, and Ohio University would receive something less than their proportion of total enrollment. I recall that generally with about 12 percent of total enrollment, Miami University would receive about 10 percent of the total available appropriation.

Once the percentage distribution for the six institutions had been agreed upon by the Inter-University Council, the fiscal officer of each institution proceeded to arrange the amount allocated to the institution in the line-item format desired by the Director of Finance for executive budget presentation. As of 1953, there were about six or seven line items for each state university: personal services, wages, supplies, equipment, travel, contract services, and printing. In addition, each fiscal officer prepared such detail about past, current, and future operations as the Department of Finance might desire.

I should add that there were three items of higher education appropriation that the Inter-University Council did not consider and that were negotiated directly between Ohio State and the Department of Finance. These were the appropriations for the cooperative agricultural extension service, for the agricultural experiment station, and for the teaching hospitals. Otherwise, the appropriations for all the instructional programs of Ohio State were handled in the same way as for the other state universities. And the procedure employed for determining the current operating appropriation was repeated in the negotiation and distribution of the capital improvements appropriations, sometimes referred to as the additions and betterments appropriation. It was state practice for the chief executive and the General Assembly to consider the capital improvements appropriation after consideration of the current operating appropriation was well under way toward its July 1 deadline. The capital improvements appropriation might not be enacted until August or September. The financing of capital improvements was a troublesome problem of state finance, and I shall return to this problem shortly.

There apparently was no time from 1939 through 1963 that the Governor and Director of Finance did not accept the Inter-University Council recommendation for the distribution of the total appropriation to higher education. There certainly was no such incident in my own personal experience from 1953 through 1963, and I never heard of any such incident as having happened in the years from 1939 to 1953. Of course, the total appropriation for higher education recommended by the Governor was never as much as the Inter-University Council wanted. And the General Assembly never appropriated more than the Governor recommended. There was one unusual occurrence in 1955 when Governor Lausche sent word to the Inter-University Council through the Director of Finance that he was willing to increase somewhat the total appropriation for higher education beyond the amount originally recommended in his executive budget. We presidents then presented the agreed-upon addition to the Committee on Finance of the House of Representatives, and with the concurrence of the Director of Finance, the Committee then increased the various appropriation line items accordingly. This increased appropriation happened only that one year, but it was a pleasant happening.

There were two good reasons why both houses of the General Assembly were disposed to accept the recommendations of the executive budget. In Ohio, the Governor enjoys the power of item veto and anytime the legislature increased an appropriation above the recommendation, there was always the danger of executive disapproval. In addition, Ohio budget law required the chief executive to submit a balanced budget or to make recommendations for the necessary tax increases to balance increased expenditures. For the General Assembly to increase appropriations, the General Assembly on its own initiative would have had to enact new taxes, and legislators were seldom if ever disposed to take this action. It was always possible for the legislature to reduce any appropriation recommendation of the Governor but such action was unusual.

It may be asked why Ohio Governors and legislators were willing to accept the distribution of the available higher education appropriation as proposed by the Inter-University Council. The explanation is simple. The alternative was for the Governor or the General Assembly to determine the relative entitlement or needs of each state university, and any such determination could not fail but to precipitate a bitter political battle. Ohio had five state universities strategically located throughout the state: one in the southeast, one in the southwest, one in the northeast, one in the northwest, and one in the exact center. Only Central State College did not fit this geographical pattern and it was necessarily recognized as a special situation. Although only Ohio State in Columbus was located in a major urban center, all others except Ohio University were located adjacent to major urban areas. Moreover, the population of Ohio was distributed fairly evenly among eight large cities and three of the four quadrants of the state. The legislative representatives of no one part of the state were sufficiently numerous or influential to dominate legislative decision-making and favor one particular institution. Despite its large size, Ohio State could not dominate the politics of Ohio because legislators from Cincinnati, Dayton, Toledo, Akron, Canton, Youngstown, and Cleveland were not disposed to be especially friendly toward Columbus. The result of these circumstances was that governors and legislators were quite content in the years from 1939 to 1963 to have the Inter-University Council of state universities determine the distribution of the higher education appropriation. The arrangement prevented bitter political strife within the General Assembly.

I do not wish to suggest by these observations that the state university presidents were satisfied with the total appropriation in support of higher education provided by executive and legislative action. On the contrary, all the presidents were continually dissatisfied. I was quite surprised myself to find in 1953 that the total appropriation of operating funds from tax revenues for six institutions enrolling about 40,000 students for the fiscal year 1953–54 came to 26 million dollars. Between fiscal 1954 and fiscal 1963 the total appropriation increased to 55.6 million dollars, but enrollments in the autumn of 1962 had risen to over 81,000 students. Ohio as a state was simply not disposed to support its public higher education on generous terms. I often asked many different persons for an explanation of this situation and I never found a satisfactory answer. It appeared to me that the wealthy social, economic, and political leaders of the State sent their sons and daughters to the major private colleges and universities of the East. Everyone was well aware that the men in the Taft family were Yale men. The state universities existed to provide educational opportunity for the sons and daughters of school teachers, preachers, the artisans, and other middle class citizens, and there was no need to spend any undue amount upon their education.

Because state appropriations were considered usually to be inadequate for the perceived income needs of each state university, as soon as a legislative session had adjourned the presidents found it necessary to go to their boards of trustees and ask for an increase in the instructional charge to students. In 1953 when I arrived at Miami University, students were charged fees of 75 dollars a semester. By 1963 these charges had risen to 200 dollars a semester. In general, the universities with the exception of Central State College endeavored to keep their fee charges fairly comparable, although there were some differences. I find from the record that in 1963 Ohio State had student fees for an academic year that were 95 dollars higher than those of Miami, while Kent State had student fees 70 dollars less.

By the early 1960s the size of student fee charges was beginning to become a political issue in Ohio, and some criticisms were being made that the state universities were squeezing all they could out of the taxpayers and were then squeezing all they could out of the students. To some extent, this complaint was justified. The response of the presidents was that if the State would increase appropriations properly, then the state universities would not have to be constantly increasing the charges to students. The politics of student fee charges were to become a major issue after I moved from Miami University to the Ohio Board of Regents.

After about five years of personal experience in the Inter-University Council, I became quite dissatisfied with our procedure for distributing the available state tax dollars among the six state-supported institutions. It was obvious that we had no criterion for this distribution except enrollment size, and it was obvious that our departures from enrollment were made in recognition of program differences without any knowledge about relative program costs. I voiced this dissatisfaction to my colleagues, and as a result the Inter-University Council in 1959 decided to undertake some instructional cost studies at all six institutions. Initially, we brought in an outside consultant to establish the framework and to guide the conduct of these studies. Later, in 1961 as I recall, the Council decided to hire a full-time executive secretary whose primary assignment would be the further development of these cost studies. We were fortunate in recruiting William B. Coulter for this position; previously he had served as the higher education analyst and liaison officer in the State Department of Finance. Later he was to join my staff in the Ohio Board of Regents and to be of inestimable assistance there. He became acting chancellor when I departed Ohio in 1972.

We never succeeded in utilizing these cost studies in the Inter-University Council. But when I went to Columbus on July 1, 1964, and was soon involved in negotiations with the Governor and Director of Finance on the size of the higher education appropriation for the biennium 1965–67, negotiations that had to be completed by December, 1964, I found these cost studies of immense value to me. I have often said that the work of the Inter-University Council before 1964 made it possible for the Ohio Board of Regents to function effectively in the appropriation arena beginning in 1964. Without these data and this background, the Board of Regents could not have undertaken its budget role.

Beginning in 1959 we in the state universities had some bitter political experiences. I shall recount part of the story here and reserve another part for telling in the next chapter. In 1958 Michael V. DiSalle, Democrat of Toledo, had been elected to the first four-year term as Governor of Ohio. The State Constitution had been amended by vote of the electorate in 1954 to lengthen the gubernatorial term from two to four years. DiSalle had defeated Governor C.

William O'Neill in his 1958 bid for reelection largely because certain conservative leaders in the State had injected
the right-to-work issue into the campaign. Labor and moderate voters had risen in their wrath to defeat the proposed
constitutional amendment, placed on the ballot by petition,
which would have outlawed the closed shop. And in the
process the voters elected a Democratic Governor and a
Democratic legislature.

In presenting his executive budget in March, 1959, Governor DiSalle proposed the first important changes in the
tax structure since 1935. In fact, the recommended changes
were quite modest. The 3 percent sales tax was to be extended to certain products not previously taxed, and the tax
was to begin with purchases above 11 cents instead of above
25 cents. In addition, the utility tax and the corporation
franchise tax were to be increased, as well as the tax on
cigarettes and other tobacco products. I believe the prices at
the state liquor stores were also to be increased in order to
produce more state revenue. These tax increases were hotly
debated in the General Assembly, and the new tax law was
not finally enacted until late in August. The political situation in the State Senate was a complicated one, since the
Governor could not count upon the support of the five
Democratic senators from Cuyahoga County (Cleveland).
Eventually, two Republican state senators had to be persuaded to vote for the tax measure. One of these men voted
his conviction that the State had to have increased revenues; the other no doubt voted his convictions also, but his
convictions were reinforced by some bargaining that involved the state universities. The senator wanted a branch
of Ohio State located in his home town, although the city
was geographically closer to Bowling Green than to Columbus. We presidents agreed that a branch was desirable in
the city involved, but we had to juggle our previously
agreed-upon boundary lines in order to assign the city to
Ohio State.

Inevitably, I became involved as the negotiator in this instance, since the president of Ohio State could scarcely take the lead. And the result was that I had my first complete baptism in the joys of legislative lobbying. I have some very vivid recollections of that 1959 legislative session, and there are some vivid stories I could recount about that session. But the tax law was passed in late August, the appropriation bill was then immediately enacted, and the state universities received a biennial appropriation in excess of 91 million dollars compared with 74 million dollars in the biennium 1957–59.

But the aftermath of the 1959 session was to be troublesome. In the 1960 presidential election, which included the election of all members of the Ohio House of Representatives and one-half of the members of the Ohio Senate, the Republican leadership in Ohio decided to make the DiSalle tax increases of 1959 the major political issue. The existence of a business recession in 1960 and the sluggish performance of the Ohio economy during the 1950s added fuel to the conflagration. With some sense of desperation Governor DiSalle in September, 1960, opened a counterattack. He launched a series of so-called seminars throughout Ohio to explain the need for increased state revenues and the still unsatisfactory financing of badly needed services. The Governor called me and asked permission to hold his first seminar at Miami University; in addition, he wanted me to make the presentation on the still inadequate financing of higher education in Ohio. It seemed to me that I was in a very poor position to refuse either request of Governor DiSalle, and I was disposed to like the man in any event. The Governor was pleased by my arrangements at Miami and by my presentation. He decided to hold additional seminars at other state universities, but wanted me to continue to be the spokesman for the state universities. Before I knew what was happening I found myself involved in the political campaign of 1960. And before I extricated myself I was strongly identified with Governor DiSalle and the Democratic Party. No one seemed to care that I was a registered Republican.

The 1960 election was a disaster for the Democrats in Ohio. John F. Kennedy was just barely elected President of the United States, but Richard Nixon carried Ohio by 250,000 votes. More importantly for the state universities, the Republicans acquired substantial majorities in both houses of the Ohio General Assembly. In January, 1961, Governor DiSalle had to present his executive budget for the 1961–63 biennium to a hostile legislature.

Governor DiSalle decided upon two innovations in his budget presentation. He gave the General Assembly two different sets of appropriation recommendations, one based upon a balancing of income and appropriations and the other based upon "needs." In the second set of appropriation recommendations, the school foundation program, the mental health program, the welfare program, and the higher education program were all given larger amounts than in the first budget. Since these four programs amounted to over 80 percent of the appropriations from the State's General Fund, the second executive budget was considerably higher than the first. But the Governor did not accompany his higher appropriation recommendation with any recommendation for increased taxes. He said only that he wanted the General Assembly to know what he considered to be the spending needs of the state. The second innovation of Governor DiSalle was to have all department heads present in the legislative chamber when he presented his budget message. Ostensibly they were on hand to answer any questions raised by legislators. But the combined session of the two houses was adjourned immediately upon conclusion of the Governor's message. The incident served, however, to identify the State Superintendent of Public Instruction and the state university presidents with Governor DiSalle.

The Republican-controlled General Assembly was outraged by the two budget recommendations of the Governor. They finally decided to reject the executive budget entirely, and the House Finance Committee proceeded to write its own appropriation bill, the amounts set forth closely paralleling those in Governor DiSalle's first budget. Again, it was a long, hot summer before an appropriation measure was enacted into law. The biennial total for higher education from tax funds came to some 107.6 million dollars for 1961–63, compared with 91.4 million dollars in 1959–61, and compared with over 120 million dollars set forth in the Governor's second budget. The state university presidents became individually involved in the many numerous conferences and discussions that accompanied the appropriation process. My recollection is that, once again, the legislators accepted the judgment of the Inter-University Council about the distribution of the total among the six institutions.

But 1961 brought new evidence of stress for the Inter-University Council. The details are relevant in connection with the discussion of capital plant financing and with the telling of the story about the creation of the Ohio Board of Regents. Here, I would emphasize only the point that nominally all decisions of the Inter-University Council had to be made by unanimous consent of the six institutions. Any one institution at any time could veto any proposed action, even if five other institutions were in agreement. This requirement of a unanimous vote paved the way for the collapse of the Inter-University Council in 1961 in connection with capital improvement appropriations.

Financing Capital Improvements

In state and local governments the financing of capital improvements has been a major problem throughout all of this century. Dependent as they are upon state governments for a part of their physical plant, state universities have their stake in this situation. There are essentially three choices for state governments in financing capital improvements. One choice is to utilize current tax revenues to finance additions to plants, even as these same revenues are used to finance operating expenses. This plan is sometimes referred to as the "pay-as-you-go" method of financing. It is a desirable practice, but it means that a state's revenue structure must produce sufficient income to meet needed expenditures for current services and for plant improvements. Between the pressures to avoid large tax increases and the pressures for increased expenditures on current services, state and local governments often postpone needed capital improvements in favor of current services. A second choice is to finance plant improvements from revenue bonds, the charges for use of the facility then meeting the debt service requirements. Student housing and other facilities at state universities have been financed in this way, not to mention turnpikes, bridges, parks, and other state government projects. A third method is for a state or local government to borrow funds for capital improvements and then to include the debt service costs as a current operating expenditure.

As I have mentioned earlier, I was much concerned about the physical plant resources of Miami University when I arrived there in 1953. Apparently from 1885 to 1929 the State of Ohio had provided some appropriations for capital improvements at the state universities from current tax resources. Then beginning in 1931 under the impact of the depression, there came a complete cessation of capital improvement appropriations; this halt was an economy the State could immediately adopt with a minimum of political resistance. When the sales tax was enacted in 1935 there were too many current service needs in support of schools and welfare for the state government to provide any funds for capital improvements. During the

War years from 1941 to 1945 the State of Ohio accumulated a surplus in its General Fund, and this surplus was used to finance a number of needed capital improvement projects beginning in 1946, including four major projects at Miami University. The last appropriation for capital improvements from this surplus was made by the General Assembly in 1953 after I arrived at Miami.

In our discussions with Governor Frank J. Lausche in preparation for the 1955 session of the General Assembly, the state university presidents emphasized that our institutions still had extensive unmet needs for academic facilities. The Governor was sympathetic but said he saw no way in which he could use current revenues to finance any capital improvements. After the 1955 session was under way, Governor Lausche called the state university presidents together in his office one day and told us he would endorse a state bond issue for capital improvements to be built at state hospitals and state universities. He suggested a bond issue of 150 million dollars to be evenly divided between state hospitals and state universities. He proposed that the debt service be carried by an earmarked tax of one cent per package on cigarettes. In order to authorize such a bond issue, it was necessary to amend the Constitution of Ohio, since the Constitution prohibited a state debt. The procedure was for the General Assembly by a three-fifths vote to adopt a resolution proposing the specific debt as an exception to the constitutional prohibition. The proposal then had to be ratified by a majority vote of those voting on the issue at a subsequent general election.

With the Governor's endorsement, the resolution proposing this constitutional amendment was duly passed by the General Assembly in 1955. It was then left for the state universities and an association of citizens concerned with state hospitals to organize a campaign to persuade the voters to approve the amendment at the general election of November 8, 1955. I need not recount here all the efforts that went into this campaign of persuasion. I remember many meetings, many miles of travel to visit newspaper editors, many speaking engagements before Rotary Clubs and Kiwanis Clubs and similar groups, and many devices employed to acquaint persons with the proposition and to encourage their favorable response. We had to seek alumni contributions in order to finance the costs of this campaign, including newspaper advertisements and television spots. The presidents helped to organize a general citizens committee in favor of Proposition One, and direct campaign expenditures were made through this committee. It was a major political effort, and I learned several interesting political lessons as a consequence. On the morning of November 9th it was gratifying to find that Proposition One had been approved by the voters.

Governor Lausche called the General Assembly into special session early in 1956 and the first appropriations under the bond issue were made at that time. Additional appropriations were made by the General Assembly in 1957 and in 1959. In fact, the final appropriation of the 75 million for higher education was made in 1959. Thus, in addition to the other problems confronting Governor DiSalle in 1961, there was the further question of what to do about capital improvements. The state universities were pressing for more help. In 1960–61 they had over 10,000 more students than just two years before in 1958–59. And the accumulated deficit in plant resources had by no means been satisfied by the 75 million dollars of plant improvements that were being completed at that time. Governor DiSalle simply informed us that as of 1961 there would be no capital improvement appropriations.

In my discussions with Republican leaders in the General Assembly in 1961, once I had partially overcome an apparent identification with the DiSalle administration, I learned that the one cent tax per package of cigarettes enacted in

1956 was producing more income than was needed for the debt service on 150 million dollars' worth of bonds. There was further bonding capacity available for capital improvements within the limits of the earmarked tax. I found that the Speaker of the House, Roger Cloud, was interested in having the General Assembly propose another constitutional amendment in 1961 for additional state debt. In fact, Speaker Cloud called me to his office to discuss the matter. I was at the time serving as chairman of the Inter-University Council.

I learned that a young Columbus businessman, a graduate of Massachusetts Institute of Technology, had started a small electronics business and was urging state officials to invest more heavily in science and engineering facilities at the state universities in order to serve as an educational and research resource for new kinds of businesses in the state. Mr. Cloud was interested in the idea, and suggested to me that if a new state bond issue were authorized, the total of 15 million dollars should be immediately committed for improvement of science and engineering facilities at Ohio State. Then in 1963 another 15 million dollars would be available for capital improvements, and this 15 million could be divided among the other institutions, excluding Ohio State. I thought this proposition was reasonable, and I began immediately to sound out my colleagues about the matter. President John C. Baker of Ohio University informed me in no uncertain terms that he was opposed to the idea and would not approve it in a meeting of the Inter-University Council. His position was that the proposal represented an unfair advantage for Ohio State and that it was contrary to the statement of capital plant needs of all the state universities agreed to before the beginning of the 1961 legislative session. Regretfully, I returned to Speaker Cloud and told him that I could not obtain approval of his idea by the Inter-University

Council. The Speaker dropped the whole proposal, and the Inter-University Council lost a legislative friend. The consequences were to be dramatic.

I should add that in 1962 James A. Rhodes, Republican of Columbus, was elected Governor, defeating Governor DiSalle's bid for reelection to a second four-year term. Early in 1963 Governor Rhodes informed the state university presidents that he would advocate another bond issue in the amount of 250 million dollars, of which 175 million dollars was to be spent for higher education. The General Assembly adopted the proposal and it was approved at the general election of November 5, 1963. Once again we presidents were involved in a campaign of persuasion, but we were completely overshadowed this time by the direct, personal efforts of Governor Rhodes. In fact, he was largely responsible, I felt, for the successful effort. Once again a Governor called the General Assembly into special session and an appropriation bill for capital improvements was enacted. After a long pause since the last such appropriation in 1959, the state universities began to build again. But the Inter-University Council in 1964 had little to say about the distribution of the capital improvement funds. Now there was a new state government agency in existence to coordinate higher education planning and budgeting, an Ohio Board of Regents.

Conclusion

As I conclude this first chapter about political experiences in Ohio from 1953 to 1964, there are three generalizations I would make. Obviously, there is much more to the whole story of state university and state government relationships in these years than I have been able to tell here. I do not wish to suggest that a state university president is exclusively preoccupied with state government relationships. He has other tasks to perform and other issues to resolve. And yet as I have gone back and reread the eleven annual reports that I submitted to the Board of Trustees of Miami University between 1954 and 1964, I find that a considerable part of them was devoted to discussions of financing current operations and capital plant, issues involving relationships with state government. The times were such that these issues were vital concerns of institutional leadership.

As I rethink the political objectives of the state universities in Ohio in these years from 1953 to 1964, I believe that they were primarily two. One objective was institutional autonomy. The other objective was adequate financial support from the state government. The state university presidents were well aware that the two objectives were not mutually consistent one with the other. The task was to make them as consistent as human ingenuity and effort could devise.

The Inter-University Council of Ohio was a device for strengthening university autonomy by voluntary cooperation and by the avoidance of internecine political competition. At the same time when the state universities gave up the privilege of separate political endeavor each for its own advantage, these universities bound themselves together in a common approach to state government on appropriation and other issues. The arrangement could endure only so long as all institutions worked together in a sense of mutual good will and mutual advantage. And the arrangement could endure only so long as the political leadership thought it was responsive to the needs of the state. By 1961 these prerequisites of successful operation had been lost.

What does a state university mean by autonomy? I have often asked myself and others this question. I am convinced that political autonomy and academic freedom are not the same thing, although they are interrelated. Academic freedom is the privilege of the faculty member to teach and to conduct research according to his or her own standards of professional competence, as formulated and enforced by faculty members in their collegial capacity. Institutional autonomy is something different: the privilege to determine what instructional objectives to pursue, what instructional programs to offer, what students to admit, what procedures of instruction to practice, and what standards of performance to maintain. In effect, the concept of institutional autonomy for a state university says to a state government: give us the support we say we need and then leave us alone.

Autonomy for a state university is a great idea. The trouble is that the concept of autonomy is not realistic when a state university is continually seeking more state government financial support. What is adequate financial support for a state university? I don't know any way to answer this question except to say that adequate financial support means more state support this year than last year. The rub is how much more? The answer of the political representatives of the voters is that there is no need for state universities to have all the support they want. The answer of political representatives is that there has to be some degree of political responsibility and political accountability for state universities.

I am of course well aware that the traditional organizational arrangement within our states to achieve both autonomy and accountability for state universities is through the device of a board of trustees. The difficulty with this tradition is that it is at best only partially effective as an organizational arrangement. The composition of a board of trustees can be changed over a period of time. But whatever their composition, boards of trustees are generally made up of laymen who are not familiar with or competent to resolve troublesome educational issues of goals, objectives, programs, and procedures. Higher education has become too highly professional for the layman to substitute his judgment for faculty judgment. The board of trustees can advise faculties and on occasion veto their actions for good and sufficient cause. But boards of trustees can't perform the work of a university.

The basic fault of a state university board of trustees, however, is the same as the limitation that applies to the president of a state university. Both have an institutional point of view. Both are expected to do all they can to advance the best interests of the university they serve. It is entirely appropriate for them to do so. Yet the best interests of a particular state university at a particular time may or may not coincide with the best interests of a state government insofar as higher education is concerned. Should a state university be permitted to start a college of medicine on its own volition and then expect the state government to meet the bill? Should a state university decide a policy on access to higher education regardless of state government policy on this subject? I think the answer to these and similar questions is no. There is a limit to the autonomy of a state university to determine its own policies, programs, and financing. The problem has been how to fix these limits, and especially what administrative devices to create to advise about and to enforce these limitations.

These observations lead me in turn to the question about just what political resources a state university enjoys. I have asked myself this question for over twenty years, and I still do not have a satisfactory answer. The only answer I have is that a state university has such political resources as public good will affords. I early learned that the public schools have done much better than public universities in building political resources. The local nonpartisan election of school board members, the parent-teachers association, the association of teachers—and the large number of persons thus brought together in a common interest—have all combined to provide political clout for the public schools.

Where is the corresponding political clout for state universities? I could not find it among alumni; one of my major political opponents in the Ohio General Assembly was a Republican legislator who was a graduate of Miami University. I could not find it among faculty members; most of them were very little interested in mutual political activity and united support of a political leader. I could not find it among students, although students could be an important political interest group if they wanted to behave the way an interest group must behave in order to be effective. I could not find political support for higher education among other interest groups, except from local chambers of commerce when they wanted educational services to promote business location and expansion in their individual communities. State universities are not effective developers of political power. And thereby hangs the remainder of this political tale.

2

The Struggles for Organizational Expression of a State Interest in Higher Education: 1955–1963

THE OHIO BOARD OF REGENTS WAS CREATED AS A STATE board of higher education by House Bill No. 214 of the 105th Ohio General Assembly, passed by both houses and approved by the Governor to be effective September 20, 1963. The new law enacted by the General Assembly and the Governor became Chapter 3333 of the Revised Code of Ohio. Behind this simple statement of legislative action lay a considerable history, as is the case with any important piece of legislation.

The immediate story begins in 1961. I have already mentioned that 1961 was a troublesome year in Ohio with a Democratic governor and a Republican legislature at odds with each other about the desirable level of financing for state activities, including higher education. Within the Inter-University Council, 1961 was also a bitter year. On four different matters of major importance, a considerable difference of position had arisen between the representatives of the six state institutions of higher education. These differences were such that they involved more than just institutional rivalries; they involved the State of Ohio as well. Differences that involve issues of state-wide public policy necessarily cry out for political resolution. And that is what happened in Ohio.

The four important differences that separated the state universities as of 1961 were: (1) the allocation of a capital improvement appropriation if additional state debt were to be authorized; (2) the development of doctoral degree programs by state universities other than The Ohio State University; (3) the kind of desirable arrangement for long-term planning of higher education in Ohio; and (4) the status and role of the Inter-University Council in state planning for higher education.

I have previously reviewed the disagreement that developed during the 104th General Assembly in 1961 about the allocation of proposed additional capital improvement financing. It is sufficient here simply to state again that the inflexible political position of the Inter-University Council on this matter created adverse political reactions within the General Assembly and prompted the beginnings of a search for new state government mechanisms in the field of higher education administration. The other three areas of disagreement require some discussion here.

Doctoral Education

The matter of education at the doctoral degree level became an important concern for all state universities in the 1950s. The state universities in Ohio were no exception. As far back as 1906 there had been a bitter battle in The Ohio General Assembly about the appropriate role and mission for Ohio University, Miami University, and the Ohio State University. The issue had been raised by William Oxley Thompson, president of Ohio State, who interestingly enough had been president of Miami University from 1891 to 1899. Upon his arrival at Columbus, where he was president until retirement in 1925, Thompson became an enthusiastic, vigorous, and effective promoter for Ohio State. In large part, he provided the leadership that made Ohio State a major university in the nation. But in the exercise of this leadership Thompson had one vital flaw. He did not see Ohio State as a part of a state system of higher education; he saw Ohio State rather as a rival and competitor for state support with Ohio University and Miami University.

President Thompson pushed the development of Ohio State in two directions. One was in the development and expansion of professional education; under his leadership, Ohio State absorbed two separate medical schools in Columbus, began a college of law, and started a college of education. The other was in the development and expansion of graduate education, especially at the doctoral degree level. It was during the Thompson years that Ohio State was invited into that select membership which constitutes the Association of American Universities. But these efforts of President Thompson had to be accomplished in the face of the niggardly attitude of Ohio government about the financial support of state sponsored higher education. Cleveland had two outstanding institutions of higher education, both privately sponsored: Western Reserve University and Case Institute of Technology. Cincinnati, Akron, and Toledo had municipal universities which these cities were supporting. Thompson had to develop Ohio State in Columbus with funds provided by the Governor and General Assembly of Ohio.

For some reason, President Thompson decided that Ohio University and Miami University were roadblocks in his plans for Ohio State. Accordingly, he endorsed a proposal that would have restricted all state government support for Ohio University and Miami University to teacher education. How he expected the undergraduate education in the arts and sciences to be supported was not clear. In any event, Ohio University and Miami University mustered all the political support they could arouse, and a compromise law was enacted which directed Ohio State to provide professional education and the other two universities to offer arts and sciences and teacher education. Then in 1910, as I have mentioned earlier, the General Assembly provided for the creation of two new teachers colleges. The 1906 legislation was largely forgotten in the 1920s and 1930s, even if President Thompson's attack was not. When I came to Miami in 1953, I discovered that no building there was named for Thompson and that no one connected with Miami had a good word for Thompson. His statue might loom large on the Ohio State campus, as it does, but his name was anathema in Oxford and Athens, Ohio.

When the Inter-University Council was organized in 1939, the constitution provided that only Ohio State would offer educational programs at the doctoral degree level. The other four state universities were primarily involved in undergraduate education in the arts and sciences, business, teacher education, and the fine arts, although Ohio University also had a college of engineering. In the 1930s these institutions began to offer programs at the master's degree level, but voluntarily they agreed not to expand at the doctoral level.

In 1956, as he was retiring from office, President Howard L. Bevis of Ohio State remarked in a rather casual way at a meeting of the Inter-University Council that the time was probably at hand when the other state universities should begin to develop doctoral degree programs. I don't know what motivated President Bevis to make this comment. In any event, President John C. Baker of Ohio University not only expressed gratification with the position of President Bevis, but also announced that Ohio University was proceeding to develop doctoral degree programs. Later, he argued that the Board of Trustees of Ohio University had never approved the Inter-University Council charter of 1939 and had not pledged itself to refrain from the development of doctoral degree programs. Subsequently, President Ralph G. McDonald of Bowling Green State University let it be known that Bowling Green intended also to develop doctoral degree programs.

Threatened with a series of difficulties, including the obvious intention of several state universities not to observe whatever promises they had made about instructional programs in 1939, the Inter-University Council wrote a new constitution and set of by-laws in 1961. This new constitution became effective on January 5, 1962. This time the constitution pledged the state universities to act together on such matters as student tuition fees, admission policies, the creation of branches, faculty salaries, appropriation requests, legislative matters, and educational programs and degrees. But the constitution exempted from Council jurisdiction any branch operations or educational programs in effect as of January 5, 1962. Thus, the state universities in effect broke the old constitution in 1956 and in writing a new constitution in 1961 covered in all the educational actions, especially the doctoral degree programs and branch campuses, developed in the interval.

It is a fair conclusion to state that for five years in the 1950s the Inter-University Council simply was not operative in the areas of branch operations and the inauguration of new Ph.D. programs.

Long-Term Planning

Another problem arose for the Inter-University Council as the years of the 1950s unfolded. This was the problem of preparing for the years of the 1960s. As I have mentioned, I was director of a major study on higher education between the years 1949 and 1952. That study reflected the concerns of college and university presidents as I talked with them during those years. These concerns primarily were: enrollment losses as the veterans' bulge worked its way through the higher education pipeline, the prospects for continued federal government support of research, fear of large-scale drafting of manpower because of the Korean War, the impact of Korean War inflation, the admission standards and instructional objectives of the future, and how to obtain the income to upgrade the status of higher education in American society. But there was one problem I never heard mentioned in those years and one I wasn't smart enough to foresee for myself: the impact of the new birth rate upon higher education enrollments in the 1960s.

In 1953 the American Association of Collegiate Registrars and Admissions Officers published a little pamphlet prepared by Ronald B. Thompson, registrar of The Ohio State University. This pamphlet was entitled *Estimating College Age Population Trends, 1940–1970.* The pamphlet made a simple point: in the six years from 1947 through 1952 there were one million more births each year than the average number of births each year in the ten-year period from 1937 through 1946. The persons born in 1947 would be 18 years of age, the customary age of college entry, in 1965; those born in 1952 would be ready for college in 1970. Actually, the number of births continued to rise to a figure of 4.2 million persons in 1960 and has fallen to around 3 million births in 1973, the lowest number since 1945. Youth born in 1960 will be of college age in 1978.

Thompson pointed out that the college age population would be distributed in different proportions in various states. He foresaw that in some nine states the college age population by 1970 would be 100 percent larger than it was in 1953; in some thirteen states the increase would be from 75 to 100 percent; and in another eleven states the increase would be from 50 to 75 percent. The increase for Ohio in the college age population was estimated to be 95 percent, or almost a doubling.

I should pause here to make a very important observation about a factor which Thompson purposefully omitted from his original calculations: the propensity of eighteen-year-olds to enroll in higher education. If a fixed proportion of all eighteen-year-olds enrolled in college, then entering enrollments would fluctuate with the number of eighteen-year-olds in the population. But a far more important factor for higher education enrollments during the

1960s was the *proportion* of young people enrolling in college. It appears that we reached a peak in 1967 or 1968 when about 44 percent of all males at eighteen and nineteen years of age enrolled in college; that proportion has now fallen to around 38 percent; for women the proportion has been stable at around 34 percent for the past six or seven years. By way of contrast, I may mention that about 12 percent of all eighteen-year-olds went to college in 1929, the year when I graduated from high school and enrolled at DePauw University.

The Thompson report of 1953, revised and reissued in 1954, suddenly made the higher education world aware that there might be a "tidal wave of students" threatening to inundate our colleges and universities by 1964. What did American colleges and universities intend to do about the prospect? In Ohio, the forecast of this tidal wave was brought to the attention of the presidents of the Ohio College Association in 1954 by President Bevis of Ohio State. The Ohio College Association was an organization of the accredited colleges and universities in Ohio, both public and private. Although including many different sections, the policy-making section of the Association over the years has been that of the presidents. In 1955 the Association president appointed a Committee on the Expanding Student Population with President Bevis as chairman and composed of six other members, including this author. President Bevis negotiated a grant of $7500 from the Ford Foundation, and at a special meeting on September 29, 1955, the Ohio College Association voted a special assessment of a matching $7500 and authorized the Committee to undertake a study of desirable action.

The result was the publication in late 1956 of a study prepared by John Dale Russell entitled *Meeting Ohio's Needs in Higher Education.* I shall not attempt here to review the findings or proposals put forth in the Russell report. It is sufficient to say that John Dale Russell anticipated the

major social and public policy issues that were to agitate
higher education and government in Ohio over the next
fifteen years: open or limited access to higher education,
equality of access to higher education, the expansion of
existing institutions or the creation of new institutions such
as community colleges, the adequacy of opportunities for
professional education and especially for medicine, the
needs for expanded opportunities for graduate education,
the possible development of technical education, and the
financing of needed expansion. On one matter John Dale
Russell was duly cautious: who should take the leadership
in developing the plans to meet Ohio's needs in higher
education.

In 1956 Ohio elected a new governor, C. William O'Neill,
Republican of Marietta. President Baker of Ohio University was on terms of especially friendly relationship with
Governor O'Neill, and as I recall the circumstances President Baker was influential in persuading the Ohio College
Association to recommend to the incoming Governor the
creation of another study group, this time under state government auspices. In any event, on March 11, 1957, Governor O'Neill appointed the Ohio Commission on Education
Beyond the High School made up of twelve members, with
President Baker as chairman. The commission included
three public university presidents (two state university presidents and one municipal university president), five presidents of private colleges and universities, and four prominent citizens of the state. The work of the commission was
financed with money contributed from private sources.
What was new in the work of the Baker Commission was the
source of its activity; the sponsorship had now been transferred to the State of Ohio. President Baker acknowledged
that the Inter-University Council was not the appropriate
sponsor, because the private institutions, the municipal institutions, and the general public needed to be drawn into
the study effort.

Although the Baker Commission report is officially dated December, 1958, I recall that in fact the report was not actually published until around March or April, 1959. In the meantime, as I have mentioned earlier, Governor O'Neill was defeated for reelection in November, 1958, and Michael V. DiSalle, Democrat of Toledo, was elected Governor. The Baker Commission set forth four so-called "basic conclusions": (1) that only moderate enrollment increases would occur up to 1963 and that there was still time to prepare for large-scale increases; (2) that all college administrators and faculties should be encouraged to plan changes and expansion; (3) that future planning should be continuous; and (4) that an interim commission for higher education planning should be established by state government. The Baker Commission presented fourteen "basic principles" as the foundation upon which its recommendations were built, and set forth a considerable number of recommendations organized under the headings of quality in education, the need for more and better paid college teachers, the need for additional facilities (especially two-year institutions and a state institution in the Cleveland area), improvements in engineering education, the expansion of graduate education, the expansion of medical education and the creation of a new medical school, the development of a student aid program, and establishment of a state interim commission on education beyond the high school to be composed of nine members appointed by the Governor and confirmed by the Senate.

I think it is fair to make two observations about the Baker Commission. The recommendations of the Commission were more specific and far-reaching than those set forth by the Russell Report in 1956. This circumstance is understandable, because the Baker Commission began with the Russell Report and saw its assignment as undertaking to set forth the actions required to meet the higher education needs sketched in the earlier study. The second comment I would make is that the agenda of recommendations proposed by the Baker Commission in effect became the agenda of action for the Ohio Board of Regents after 1963. The Baker Commission was not yet ready in 1959 to endorse the creation of a state board of higher education. It did recommend the establishment by law of an interim state government body for a four-year period to develop further details of action for consideration by the Governor and General Assembly.

Governor DiSalle and the Ohio General Assembly in 1959 enacted legislation that created an Interim Commission on Education Beyond the High School for a period ending on March 1, 1964. In addition, another bill was passed that authorized a survey of medical education, including consideration of the necessity and desirability of establishing additional state medical colleges in Ohio. The Interim Commission was made up of nine members. The Governor appointed three members from the General Assembly, and as the other six members named President Baker of Ohio University, two presidents of private colleges, the director of the Department of Finance as his personal representative, and two prominent citizens, one of whom, Mr. Charles W. Ingler, had previously been director of the Legislative Reference Service in Ohio. The Commission was provided with a small budget for its activities in 1959–61. In the spring of 1960 Governor DiSalle asked the Interim Commission to conduct the survey of medical education authorized by the General Assembly.

In the meantime, the General Assembly in 1959 passed a bill enabling a county government to establish a community college, with both capital and operating costs to be shared by the state government. Governor DiSalle vetoed this bill because no provision had been made by the General Assembly to appropriate any funds to carry out the state obligation. It seems likely to me that there were other factors involved in this veto, including the failure of the state senators from Cuyahoga County to support the Governor's tax program.

During 1960 the Ohio Interim Commission devoted its energies especially to the preparation of new legislation making possible the creation of community colleges in Ohio. The pressure for such legislation came particularly from the Cleveland area. Indeed the proposal for a community college in Cleveland had been made as far back as in 1952, by the then Superintendent of Cleveland Schools, Dr. Mark Schinerer. While still on the faculty at Columbia University, I had served as a consultant to a group set up in Cleveland in 1952–53 to consider the desirability of new developments in the area's higher education institutions. The group decided that no new public institution was needed in or near Cleveland at that time. But we also said that this conclusion should be reviewed at the end of the 1950s. The Baker Commission of 1958 identified what it termed "the Cleveland problem," and the immediate solution appeared to be the establishment of a public community college. The Ohio Interim Commission therefore undertook to prepare authorizing legislation, which could be considered again by the General Assembly in 1961.

Actually, the General Assembly in 1961 enacted three separate and very important pieces of legislation affecting the organization of public higher education in Ohio. One measure authorized county governments to create community colleges, subject to the approval of a new state agency, a state community college board set up by the law. A second measure authorized school boards to create technical institutes offering a postsecondary program in technical education, and a third measure made it possible for a county to establish a university branch district to help finance facilities for a state university branch. The sponsor of all three of these measures was a Republican state senator from Lima, Ohio, Ross Pepple, who was serving on the Interim Commission on Education Beyond the High

School. Governor DiSalle signed all three bills, and thus a pattern of two-year institutions was established, which was to prove troublesome to the Board of Regents after 1963.

I find little evidence that the Ohio Interim Commission was particularly active during the legislative session of 1961 or during the whole year. Its major attention appears to have been concentrated upon getting the study started on the subject of Ohio's needs in medical education. This study was conducted by Dr. John W. Patterson, then vice-chancellor for medical affairs at Vanderbilt University, assisted by Dr. Gordon H. Scott of Wayne State University and Dr. John B. Truslow of the University of Texas. I should mention that in 1961 the Ohio General Assembly also created a new state government agency, the Ohio Higher Education Assistance Commission, to operate a state student loan guarantee program.

As of December 31, 1961, President Baker retired at Ohio University. In addition, one of the public members of the Interim Commission, Mr. Ralph M. Besse of Cleveland, had been appointed by Governor DiSalle as chairman of the new state community college board. Mr. Besse therefore resigned from the Interim Commission. The other public member, Mr. Ingler of Dayton, had recently joined the top management staff of the National Cash Register Company and indicated that he could no longer continue to serve as chairman. In January, 1962, the Director of Finance informed me that Governor DiSalle proposed to appoint me as a member of the Ohio Interim Commission on Education Beyond the High School and that the members of the Commission would then elect me to serve as chairman. It was at best an empty honor. For the biennium 1961–63 the General Assembly had refused to appropriate any funds for a staff of the Commission; this action I understood was an expression of displeasure with the position of President Baker on the matter of the proposal for capital improvements financing.

During 1962 as chairman of the Interim Commission I gave my attention to two matters. The first obligation was to complete the medical education study. On December 28 the Interim Commission did issue a report recommending an expansion of the College of Medicine at Ohio State, the creation of a new medical college in Toledo, and the opening of negotiations with the University of Cincinnati for state support and enrollment expansion of its College of Medicine. In addition, with the assistance of a staff associate paid for by Miami University, I reviewed all of the issues in state planning for higher education as these had emerged between 1954 and 1962. This effort resulted in the issuance by me of two papers that were not necessarily endorsed by my colleagues and that set forth major higher education matters requiring some kind of state government resolution.

At the general election in November, 1962, James A. Rhodes was elected Governor. I persuaded my colleagues on the Interim Commission that although the Commission had one more year of statutory life, we should submit our resignations to the new Governor. We all did so on January 14, 1963. I argued that the new Governor who had proposed a new organization for higher education in Ohio during his gubernatorial campaign should not be encumbered by our existence while the General Assembly considered his recommendations. And in any event, we didn't have anything more to do.

I tell this story of informal and largely ineffective efforts at state planning for higher education between 1954 and 1962 in some detail for two reasons. For one thing, it is instructive to review the evolution of these efforts. First, the Ohio College Association in 1955 set up a study group to review the status of higher education resources in Ohio to meet the needs of the 1960s. The Russell Report clearly indicated that some drastic actions would be necessary. Then Governor O'Neill on his own executive initiative in

1957 set up a Commission on Education Beyond the High School to develop proposals to meet the needs set forth in the Russell Report. The Baker Commission of Governor O'Neill gave way to an Ohio Interim Commission on Education Beyond the High School authorized by law passed by the Ohio General Assembly and approved by Governor DiSalle in 1959. But the political battles of these years overshadowed any effort at state planning and an effective relationship between planning and state government was still to be established.

My second reason for reviewing this story is to emphasize that the Inter-University Council of Ohio during these years had ceased to be an agency presumably concerned with meeting Ohio's needs for public higher education. The planning function, if indeed the Inter-University Council had ever exercised it, had been transferred to another arena, to a series of *ad hoc* bodies set up apart from the Council. It is my own opinion that the Inter-University Council never was a planning agency; it was a fairly effective budget agency during most of the years from 1939 to 1961, but it had not undertaken any actual planning studies. When the critical problems of the 1950s arose, the members of the Inter-University Council were satisfied to have the planning initiative exercised elsewhere.

The Creation of the Ohio Board of Regents

In order to tell the story of House Bill No. 214 of the 105th Ohio General Assembly in 1963, I must return again to events in 1961. As I have recounted earlier, a major breakdown in the consensus with which the Inter-University Council had previously functioned occurred when President Baker of Ohio University refused to accept the proposal of the Speaker of the Ohio House of Representatives for financing additional capital improvements for higher education. Perhaps other presidents would have rejected the proposal also. Since one negative vote was sufficient to reject any proposition in the Council, there was no point in proceeding further.

Another event occurred in 1961 besides the continuing conflict about doctoral programs that indicated the growing tension within the Inter-University Council as a coordinating device. The DiSalle Administration, speaking through the Director of Finance, James Maloon, proposed that the Inter-University Council be given statutory authority by the Ohio General Assembly to carry out the work it was doing, especially in the area of state appropriations for higher education. Since 1939 the Council had operated as a voluntary, self-designated arrangement. Yet it had also exercised very real power in state government in terms of the distribution of appropriations among the six state-supported institutions.

I assumed that this proposal from Director Maloon reflected some uneasiness about the extent of the Council's *de facto* authority exercised without any statutory basis of any kind. In any event, for this or other reasons, the Department of Finance drafted a bill to establish the Inter-University Council of Ohio as a legally authorized agency to advise the Governor and the General Assembly on governmental matters affecting higher education and especially on matters of appropriations. The bill was presented to the Inter-University Council for its consideration and endorsement. I urged my colleagues to approve the proposal and to work for its enactment. The other presidents and the trustee members of the Council took a different point of view. They argued that a law establishing an Inter-University Council would make the Council an instrumentality of state government rather than an agency of the state universities themselves. The Council voted not to approve, the president and the trustee member of Miami University dissenting.

I well remember the meeting in Columbus with Director Maloon and his associate, John Stanley, when the final discussion and the vote on the proposed legislation was taken. With some display of anger and frustration, Mr. Maloon and Mr. Stanley left our conference room at Ohio State. At the doorway, Mr. Maloon paused for one final word. He would not press the matter further, he stated, but he wanted to give the Council a final word of warning. The next time the subject of a state agency for higher education was brought up for consideration, Mr. Maloon declared, the Inter-University Council would not be consulted. Next time, Mr. Maloon predicted, the state universities would be told about state organization, not asked. I don't know about my colleagues, but I never forgot that scene. And Mr. Maloon turned out to be a prophet of things to come.

Sometime during the autumn of 1961, I am told, Mr. Cloud, as Speaker of the House of Representatives, attended a conference of state legislators held under the auspices of the Council of State Governments. Here Mr. Cloud learned that in 1961 the Illinois General Assembly had created a board of higher education as an agency of state government. Furthermore, he discovered that there were several state governments that at that time had state boards of higher education, some going back to the 1930s. When Mr. Cloud returned to his office in Columbus, he decided to ask the Legislative Service Commission, the principal staff arm of the Ohio General Assembly, to make a study of state coordination of higher education. Since the Speaker is *ex officio* a co-chairman of the Service Commission, the Speaker's request led to immediate action by the Commission to authorize the study. This episode reveals how dangerous it is to let legislators in one state find out what is going on in other states.

The Legislative Service Commission carried on its study during the calendar year 1962. The staff researcher was James M. Furman, who in 1963 went to Dayton to become director of Community Research, Inc. In 1964 I persuaded Mr. Furman to return to Columbus as my principal associate on the staff of the Ohio Board of Regents and as the legislative liaison officer for the Board. He served in out-standing fashion in this role until 1970, when he went to the State of Washington as the first executive coordinator of the Council on Higher Education created by the Washington State Legislature in 1969.

The Legislative Service Commission report on *Coordination of Higher Education* was not published until January, 1963. I have reason to believe that an early draft of the report was available for legislative review by the autumn of 1962 during the gubernatorial election. When the report was published, it was quite critical of the failures of the Inter-University Council, pointing particularly to the de-velopment of doctoral degree programs at Ohio University, Kent State, and Bowling Green, as examples of separate rather than planned action. The report mentioned also that the two governmental efforts to date at state-wide planning, the O'Neill Commission and the Interim Commission, had not been successful endeavors. The need for state planning and coordination was presented in terms of meeting the unprecedented enrollment demands of the 1960s. There followed a review of organizational arrangements for state-wide planning and coordination in other states. The report concluded with this statement:

> Past experience with voluntary coordination in this state indicates that it does not prepare or equip the state to meet the innumerable existing and impending challenges to its system of higher education. The establishment of a formal state-wide planning agency merits strong consideration as a means to improve coordination.

During his campaign for the office of Governor, James A. Rhodes issued a statement entitled *Blue Print for Brain Power*. In this statement Mr. Rhodes declared that it was a matter of urgent economic and cultural importance for Ohio to advance and improve its public structure for higher education. If elected governor, Mr. Rhodes declared that he would put higher education high on his agenda for state government action, including the establishment of a state board of regents to plan and guide this development. I believe that Mr. Cloud had a great deal to do with the contents of this statement. On November 6, 1962, Mr. Rhodes was elected Governor. He was inaugurated as Governor on January 14, 1963. A short time later the presidents of the state universities learned that a bill was being drafted in the Governor's office to create an Ohio Board of Regents.

Concerned and alarmed, the Inter-University Council convened two or three times to discuss its response to the proposal to establish a state board of higher education. In the absence of any very definite knowledge about the contents of the measure, there was little the Council could do except to express its general fear that the new board would interfere with institutional autonomy. In some fashion, which I do not now remember in detail, I learned in February that I might be permitted to see the draft of the bill as it was then being prepared. To the best of my knowledge, no other state university president was extended this privilege, although it seems quite probable that President Fawcett of Ohio State may have had the same opportunity.

On two occasions, I visited a prominent attorney, a former trustee of Ohio State and a political associate of Governor Rhodes, who was drafting the proposed bill. I was reassured in the first place to learn that the contemplated board of regents was to be a state-wide planning and coordinating agency, not a state-wide governing board. The authority vested in the new board appeared to be quite similar to that contained in the 1961 law enacted in Illinois. I suggested several changes in language to make it clear that the new board would be concerned with the appropriation of state funds for current operations and for capital improvements at the state universities and that the authority of boards of trustees to finance auxiliary services and auxiliary service facilities was not included in the jurisdiction of the Board of Regents. My suggestions were accepted; indeed, the language I wrote to make this distinction clear was incorporated into the draft measure.

As I recall, House Bill No. 214 was introduced into the Ohio House of Representatives with the sponsorship of the Republican leadership in March, 1963. Hearings were promptly scheduled. Now the state universities were confronted with the hard decision whether or not publicly to oppose the bill. At a meeting of the Inter-University Council, I made my own position emphatic. Under no circumstances would I appear in opposition to the bill. I was convinced that the Inter-University Council was not and would not become an appropriate instrument of state government planning and coordination, and I was equally convinced that the succession of temporary state agencies under Governor O'Neill and Governor DiSalle had proven ineffective. It was time to have a continuing agency of state government with some degree of authority to get things done, and 1964 and the tidal wave of students were only one year away from us.

The presidents and trustees of the state universities making up the Inter-University Council were caught in a fateful dilemma. On the one hand, they were confronted by a Republican Governor and a strongly Republican General Assembly who appeared to be working together in close harmony. Moreover, the Governor had endorsed a bond issue to finance higher education facilities far beyond the wildest expectations of the state universities. And several of the trustees included prominent Republican leaders who would be placed in an embarrassing position indeed were they now to appear publicly to oppose a major item in the legislative program of the new Republican Governor. On the other hand, all of the presidents and trustees, except for myself, were exceedingly fearful of a new state board of higher education. They foresaw institutional autonomy irrevocably lost. I was more concerned that something be done to provide resources for the tidal wave of students approaching our shore.

I well remember how two trustees, one from Ohio University and one from Ohio State, came to see me informally to tell me that I was the one president who could in the existing set of circumstances prevent the passage of House Bill 214 if I were to make the effort behind the political scene. I declined both the flattery and the suggestion. I had grave doubts that I possessed any such political influence. And I suspected that I was being cast in the role of a sacrificial lamb. I saw no reason why I should accept their temptation.

Soon after the introduction of House Bill 214, Speaker Cloud asked the university presidents to meet informally in his office behind closed doors to discuss the bill with him and the Republican members of the House Education Committee, whose chairman was Representative Harold W. Oyster from Marietta. We six presidents appeared as requested, were quite cautious in our comments, and indicated our desire to appear before the Committee neither in favor nor in opposition to the measure. The six of us were unanimous in this position. We expressed our concerns about the way in which a new state board of higher education might operate, but we also pledged our cooperation with the new board if the General Assembly should see fit to enact the legislation. The Speaker and the Education Committee members expressed appreciation for our position, declared that there was no intention to be punitive toward any of the state universities, and offered to consider any language changes which would make clear that the new board was not intended to displace the existing boards of trustees.

With this meeting, the state university presidents retired from the fray, concentrated our attention upon obtaining voter approval of the huge bond issue to be voted upon in November, and left House Bill No. 214 to wend its way through the General Assembly. The bill was passed by both houses on June 13, 1963, and was approved by the Governor on June 21 to become effective on September 20, 1963. Ohio now had a state board of higher education.

The Provisions of House Bill 214

House Bill No. 214 of the 105th Ohio General Assembly created an Ohio Board of Regents consisting of nine members appointed by the Governor with the advice and consent of the Senate. The members were required to be residents of the state who possessed "an interest in and knowledge of higher education." No member might be a trustee, officer, or employee of any public or private college or university. The terms of service were nine years, the terms of three members expiring every three years. No one who served a full term of nine years might be reappointed. The members were to serve without compensation but were to be reimbursed for necessary expenses incurred in the conduct of board business.

The Board of Regents was authorized to appoint a director to serve at its pleasure and to prescribe his duties. The director was to be the administrative officer of the board and responsible for selecting and appointing employees and staff, subject to approval of the board. The law stated that the director must be a "person qualified by training and experience to understand the problems and needs of the state in the field of higher education and to devise programs, plans, and methods of solving the problems and meeting the needs."

The authority conferred upon the Board was set forth in fifteen clauses. These included authority to make studies of state policy in higher education and to formulate a master plan, to report annually to the Governor and the General Assembly on the findings of its studies, to approve or disapprove the establishment of new branch campuses and other two-year campuses, to recommend needed instructional programs, to approve or disapprove all new degrees and new degree programs at all state-assisted institutions of higher education, to conduct studies for the state-assisted institutions, to make recommendations to the Governor and General Assembly about the appropriation needs of state-assisted institutions of higher education "in close cooperation with the director of finance," to appoint advisory committees, to seek the cooperation and advice of the officers and trustees of state-assisted institutions, and to recommend to state-assisted institutions the elimination of any programs because of duplication or other "good and sufficient cause."

The Ohio Community College Board established in 1961 was abolished and all of its authority was transferred to the new Ohio Board of Regents. In addition, the Board of Regents was to be the designated state agency for carrying out federal government programs in higher education. The law also specified certain actions which the boards of trustees of a state-assisted institution might not take without the approval of the Board of Regents; these were basically two in number, the creation of branch campuses and the establishment of new degree programs. The institutions were also required to submit financial information to the Board of Regents in such form as the board might prescribe, and to cooperate with the Board in supplying other desired information. Finally, the law declared that except as expressly provided therein nothing in the act was to be construed as depriving the governing boards of the state universities of the duties and powers conferred upon them by law in the government of the institutions under their control.

Conclusion

Before I conclude this account, I must add a few words about events after September 20, 1963. Governor Rhodes promptly appointed nine members of the Board of Regents and called them together in his office for their first meeting on September 23rd. All nine were prominent citizens, including Representative Oyster who had resigned his position as a member of the General Assembly. He was selected as the first chairman. The Board began to function with a temporary staff. It took two major actions. The Board began to look for consultants to help the Board to prepare a master plan, and in January, 1964, selected the Academy for Educational Development, an offshoot of the Ford Foundation, to undertake this task. Secondly, under the leadership of a special committee chaired by John Marshall Briley of Toledo, the Board began a search for a director. Mr. Briley, who had practiced law for many years in New York City before becoming an officer of the Owens Corning Fiberglas Company, visited the major foundations in New York City in his search for a director.

I recall that in January, 1964, at a meeting of the Inter-University Council I learned the news that the Board of Regents had decided upon the title of chancellor for its executive officer. Later, I learned that foundation executives in New York told Mr. Briley the title of director for the Board of Regents was not appropriate for an educational leader. Mr. Briley was urged to find a chancellor, and the Board had decided to request the General Assembly in 1965 to change the designation of its chief executive officer.

In February, 1964, I was asked to meet in Columbus with four members of the Board of Regents: the chairman, Mr. Briley, and the two members of Mr. Briley's selection committee. They informed me that they wished to offer me the appointment as director and chancellor of the Board, with the commitment of the Governor that the law would be changed in 1965 to provide the title of Chancellor. I should add here that such an amendment to the law was enacted in 1965. The only opposition to the change came from the independent motion picture exhibitors of Ohio, on the grounds that as President of Miami University I had permitted commercial movies to be shown in the student union building in competition with a locally owned motion picture house in Oxford.

I was surprised by the offer of the appointment. I had not expected it, had not sought it, and had expressed the opinion that someone ought to be brought in from outside the state to fill the position. In fact, at the time of the offer, unknown to others, I was in the process of negotiation with the governing board of a well-known university outside Ohio to become its president, a position that I was offered a few days later. The Ohio Regents told me that they had sought a chancellor from outside Ohio, but that their advisers had strongly urged my appointment.

The principal choice I faced was that between assuming the presidency of another state university outside Ohio and assuming the chancellorship in Ohio. For better or worse, I felt that I had committed so much energy in eleven years at Miami University to the State of Ohio that I had an obligation to go ahead with this investment. I sought two political clearances before accepting the offer of the Ohio Board of Regents. I inquired to make certain that my appointment was satisfactory to Governor Rhodes and that I would enjoy his support and confidence. I was assured on this score. Secondly, I personally asked President Fawcett of Ohio State if he would prefer that I not accept the position. I was not prepared to go to Columbus and begin at once a feud with the largest and most important state university in Ohio. President Fawcett promised me his cooperation. Thereupon, I accepted the appointment offered by the Ohio Board of Regents.

On June 30, 1964, with regret and with very fond memories, I resigned my position as President of Miami University. On July 1, 1964, I became Director and Chancellor of the Ohio Board of Regents. It was the beginning of eight exciting years.

3

State Planning for Higher Education:

1964–1972

WHEN THE OHIO BOARD OF REGENTS BEGAN TO OPERATE IN
September, 1963, circumstances were different in several
respects from those confronting the Inter-University
Council or the three study groups in the preceding eight
years. First of all, the time was at hand when substantial
enrollment increases were expected; the time for analysis
and discussion was past and the time for action had arrived.
Second, the State of Ohio now had an activist Governor and
a legislature disposed to cooperate with him. Third, the
State of Ohio now had a state board of higher education
that was a permanent agency of state government and that
had the capacity to act with or without the unanimous
approval of the six state universities. And in the fourth
place, the Board of Regents was prepared to move forward
rapidly as a planning agency.

At this point, I need to say something about my concept
of planning. Shortly after I returned to Columbia University in January, 1946, after two years on the staff of the
Social Science Research Council, one year on the staff of the
National Resources Planning Board in Washington, and
nearly four years on the staff of the Commanding General
of the Army Service Forces in the War Department, I wrote
a little book entitled *The Process and Organization of Government Planning.* Based upon my experiences and observations during these years, especially during my period of

federal government service, I endeavored to set forth my ideas about planning as a tool of administration. To my surprise, I have found that in my experience as president of a state university and as an administrator of state higher education, these ideas expressed nearly thirty years ago have retained their utility both as empirical propositions and as normative prescriptions.

I think of planning as preparation for action. To me, the important aspect of planning in any enterprise is the action that results from the process. I want to emphasize the word "action." I differentiate planning as a process from such other activities as research or the formulation of concepts of knowledge. I consider research for the development of knowledge to be a vital human endeavor. If I did not believe this, I would not have devoted most of my professional career to higher education, or have spent time in writing articles and books. But research to discover knowledge and the formulation of concepts of knowledge are not synonymous with planning. Planning may, and indeed I think should, make use of research and knowledge. Yet planning is a different process, a process for undertaking governmental or other activity.

Because planning is preparation for action, it must be practical. In other words, planning means preparing to do something that can be accomplished. As I understand the meaning of this word "practical," it involves at least three characteristics: the work to be done must be socially acceptable, the work must be technologically possible (in other words, there is a work process available to produce the desired output), and the work must be financially feasible. I could, of course, spend a good deal of time elaborating upon these three characteristics. For the present, I must be content simply with their enumeration.

In every field of human activity there is always some conflict between the practical and the ideal, between the planner and the utopian, between those persons who want

immediate action and those persons who want human behavior and human activity to achieve the most desirable
state of perfection of which the human intellect and the
humane spirit can conceive. The persons who provide us
with these visions of perfection are usually our artists, our
dreamers, our philosophers, our religious leaders. Our
world would be a far drearier world than it is if these
persons were not always in our midst, always infecting us
with an emotion of "divine discontent," as one artist once
expressed the feeling. Yet the dreamers are not necessarily
planners. They are not restrained by the chains of the
practical. The planner must be prepared to accomplish
what can be done, not what might possibly be the most ideal
of all human conditions.

In that little book to which I referred, I endeavored also
to draw a distinction between policy planning and program
planning. I still find this distinction useful. I am disposed to
think of policy planning as the resolution of major issues
entailing value judgments, major issues of social goals and
of the proper means for achieving the desired goals. Policy
planning is also concerned with how to obtain the economic
resources with which to pursue desired goals, and the setting of priorities among goals in a society of limited resources and great aspirations. Policy planning entails the
satisfaction of individual and interest group expectations,
at least to the extent that some kind of action can be decided
upon and undertaken.

Program planning is more concerned with the details of
action, once policy decisions have been made. Program
planning is concerned with particular outputs, particular
methods of work production, and particular resources
needed to produce the specified outputs. Program planning is preparing to get the job done.

Not for one minute do I wish to suggest that policy
planning is concerned with politics and program planning
is concerned with administration. Any such distinction is

for me entirely illusory. It seems to me that in the realm of social endeavor we have at least two different processes and often two differentiated divisions of work. One process is what I call policy planning, and it is usually performed by our instrumentalities of governance, our organs of decision-making. In our structure of government in this country, these organs of decision-making are the legislative, executive, and judicial branches. The other process is what I call program planning and is usually performed by our instrumentalities of work execution. In our structure of government, we call these instrumentalities of work execution administrative agencies.

Because planning is preparation for action, and because it involves practical issues of what can be accomplished as well as what ought to be accomplished, administrators must be heavily involved, I think, in both policy planning and program planning. As a professional in the field of higher education, I thought of myself first of all as a person competent to advise the Governor and the General Assembly of Ohio about what was needed, what was desirable, and what was practical in providing higher education services to the people of Ohio. But such advice entailed more than just technical competence. It involved matters of great political importance, of value judgments, of social goals. I never found a comfortable distinction between politics and professionalism in my eight years as chancellor of the Ohio Board of Regents.

In addition to this generalized view of planning as a political and administrative process, I believe two more observations are relevant at this point. One observation concerns my understanding of my personal role in relation to the nine persons who constituted the Board of Regents as a board. The other observation concerns my understanding of my relationship to the Governor and General Assembly of Ohio. Both of these relationships complicate and constrain the task of state government planning for higher education.

Insofar as I know, no thought was given in 1962 or 1963 by the political leaders of Ohio to the idea of making higher education an executive department headed by a director appointed by the Governor and serving at his pleasure. There are at least two states today that do have the position of secretary of education in a governor's cabinet, but the idea of a board of education or a board of trustees is so deeply imprinted in the governmental thinking of this country that any other arrangement is usually dismissed out of hand. That the members of a board should be appointed by the Governor with the approval of the Senate is a generally accepted proposition in public higher education in this country, although there are a few higher education boards elected by popular vote.

The idea of a board involves at least three purposes: to separate education or higher education from "politics," to delegate extensive decision-making authority to a combination of lay board and professional administrator, and to achieve some continuity in educational policy formulation. I shall comment here only about this idea of separating higher education from politics at the level of state government itself. In the sense in which I use the term politics as the process of determining basic social objectives, it is illusory to believe that any separation of higher education from politics is possible or desirable in our liberal democracy. When the idea of separation is discussed, I believe the implicit if not explicit objective is to provide some separation of the selection and appointment of professional staff from partisan political influence.

In any event, board administration is a fact of life in higher education and in elementary-secondary education. Legally, all authority vested in the Ohio Board of Regents was vested in the Board itself as a group of nine persons. That authority was not vested in the chancellor as an individual, or in the chancellor and staff of the Board as a group of professionally qualified, full-time persons continually concerned with higher education needs and resources. In practice, it was necessary, as I comprehended the situation, for me to act with a good deal of initiative and decisiveness on numerous occasions. Formal decisions were made by the Board, and not by me, and were faithfully recorded in the minutes of Board meetings, along with certain supporting papers. Informally, I discussed various problems with the Board in briefing sessions not open to the public, endeavored to anticipate emerging problems and alternative lines of action, and sought to obtain the advice of Board members. On appropriate occasions, I consulted the chairman and sometimes other board members by telephone. From time to time, I prepared memoranda and documents for all board members to read, and to react to if they were disposed to do so.

Formally, and legally, I was appointed to the position of chancellor by the Board and I was responsible to the Board for my conduct in that office. I served always on a one-year contract that was subject to nonrenewal at the end of every fiscal year, upon due notice three months in advance of June 30. Informally, I told the Board of my desire to retire in 1972 at the age of sixty over a year in advance of that date, and formally I requested retirement by the Board four months in advance of the end of the fiscal year.

In my eight years of service with the Ohio Board of Regents I was very fortunate in the kind of persons who served as members of the Board. In those eight years, the nine positions of Board membership were held by seventeen different persons; when I retired in 1972, there were only three persons who remained on the board from among the original nine members of 1963. In the eight years, there were six resignations, primarily upon the grounds of the pressure of other work. During 1965–67 when the Senate was evenly divided between Republicans and Democrats, one person failed to obtain confirmation by the Senate. And one member died of cancer. There was not a single person in the membership whom I did not come to respect and with whom I found it impossible to work. The Board met on two days every month, and we usually had an attendance of at least six of the nine members. To be sure, some members worked harder than others; most of the time only three or four persons could be counted on to read all the material distributed in advance of a meeting. The Board was disposed to permit me considerable flexibility in operation, and, although the Board and I on occasion had differences of opinion, there was no occasion when we were not able to adjust these differences.

There was never any doubt in my mind, however, that the really important decisions affecting higher education in Ohio were made by the Governor and the General Assembly. The Board of Regents had final authority to decide only certain particular questions: the location of two-year campuses, the need for new degree programs and new degrees, and the issuance of certificates of authorization to private nonprofit education corporations in accordance with predetermined standards of acceptable performance. In 1969 the General Assembly decided that the Board of Regents should give prior approval before any state university built new dormitories. And from time to time appropriation laws delegated certain duties to the Board of Regents, such as defining student eligibility for state subsidy and approving the tuition charges to students fixed by the state-supported institutions. In 1969 also, the General Assembly by law vested the operation of a student aid program in the Board of Regents.

But for the most part the real authority of the Board of Regents was simply advisory, advisory to the Governor and the General Assembly. The power to raise revenue and to appropriate funds for current operations and capital improvements rested with the Governor and General Assembly. The power to enact legislation creating new state universities, establishing a student aid program, defining the authority of higher education institutions, and fixing cer-

tain requirements of institutional behavior rested with the
Governor and General Assembly. The Board of Regents,
through its chancellor, might advise the Governor and the
General Assembly. The really important planning decisions were not made by the Board of Regents; they were
made by the chief executive and the legislature, with the
further participation of the judiciary on one or two occasions. And I want to add that this process is the way by which
I think planning decisions must be made in our kind of
society and in our kind of government.

With these observations set forth as background, I believe it may be useful to consider some of the major planning problems that confronted the Ohio Board of Regents
in the years 1964 to 1972. In this way the reality of state
government planning can be presented in terms of particular issues to be resolved and of decisions actually made. It is
impossible, to be sure, to attempt here to consider all the
kinds of concerns which the Board of Regents encountered. The big problems had been clearly forecast before
1964: access to higher education and enrollment growth,
the expansion of instructional programs, and medical education. The one problem not foreseen was the impact of
public higher education expansion upon the viability of
private higher education.

Enrollment

The first area of planning concern to the Ohio Board of
Regents was the provision of facilities to meet the enrollment demands of the 1960s. The problem of financing
these facilities will be discussed in the next chapter. Here we
are concerned with certain policies about enrollment expansion as these were developed in the Board's Master Plan
of 1966 and Master Plan of 1971.

The various studies made in the 1950s, primarily the
projections of Ronald Thompson and of the Baker Com-

mission, had predicted a rapid growth of higher education enrollment in Ohio during the decade of the 1960s. John Dale Russell in his 1956 report had used the enrollment projections of Thompson and had forecast a total enrollment of 157,000 students by 1960 and 249,000 by 1970, upon the assumption that enrollments would remain constant at about 30 percent of the college age population. The Baker Commission set forth two sets of enrollment projections, one based upon a constant proportion of the 18 through 21 year old age group and the other based upon an annual increase of 0.5 percent. Upon this second basis, the enrollment expectation for 1960 was 164,000 students, and the expectation for 1970 was 253,000 students. In its 1966 Master Plan, the Board of Regents forecast a total enrollment of 410,000 students by 1970, of which 280,000 would be enrolled in public institutions.

In Table 1, I have set forth the actual enrollment growth in Ohio's colleges and universities for the 20-year period from 1953 through 1972. From these data it will be noticed that total enrollment in 1960 came to 175,000 students, which exceeded the early forecasts, while the total enrollment in 1970 came to 373,000 students, much higher than the early forecasts but less than the projection of the Board of Regents made in 1965. It is worth noting, however, that the enrollment in public institutions in 1970 was almost exactly 280,000 students, which was the original estimate of the Board of Regents.

Indeed, it will be noted that the enrollment in Ohio's public institutions of higher education rose from 73,000 students in 1955 to 96,000 by 1960, to 174,000 by 1965, and 280,000 by 1970. From 1955 to 1960, the rate of increase was around 30 percent; from 1960 to 1965 it was around 80 percent; and from 1965 to 1970 it was around 60 percent. During these same years, enrollments in private colleges and universities expanded only modestly—a little over 30 percent between 1955 and 1960, but by less than 40 percent

TABLE 1

STUDENT ENROLLMENT
AUTUMN HEAD COUNT
OHIO'S COLLEGES AND UNIVERSITIES
1953–1972

	TOTAL	PRIVATE	PUBLIC
1953	115,429	52,333	63,096
1954	112,504	55,275	67,229
1955	132,110	59,427	72,683
1956	142,783	64,085	76,698
1957	148,782	66,809	81,973
1958	156,633	71,019	85,614
1959	164,879	74,806	90,073
1960	175,011	79,034	95,977
1961	187,792	82,719	105,073
1962	202,228	87,071	115,157
1963	221,973	93,491	128,482
1964	247,948	99,541	148,407
1965	275,773	101,841	173,932
1966	292,833	105,274	187,559
1967	317,547	95,727	221,820
1968	336,288	95,781	240,507
1969	360,037	94,505	265,532
1970	373,422	94,062	279,360
1971	382,937	92,400	290,537
1972	384,938	92,000	292,938

Source: Ohio Board of Regents, *Basic Data Series*, 1973. p. 11.

between 1960 and 1965—and these enrollments actually declined by almost 8 percent between 1965 and 1970.

As the Board of Regents began its work in 1963, it needed an enrollment strategy. There was never any real debate about what this strategy should be; it was to accommodate every high school graduate who presented himself or herself for enrollment. Ohio had a law dating from 1913 that in effect declared it to be state policy to provide open access to public higher education. I interpreted open access to mean that every high school graduate who wished to go to a public college or university should have the opportunity to do so. There may be economic, academic, and motivational barriers to higher education, but under an open access policy the high school graduate who asks for admission must be given the opportunity to enroll.

In seeking to make open access a reality, there had to be an expansion of enrollment capacity in the right places and in the right programs. Without attempting to review the issues involved in deciding what the right places and the right programs of instruction were, let me just say that the objective of the Board of Regents was to locate a two-year campus within thirty miles of every person in the state and to locate a four-year campus in all eight major urban areas of the state. In the process, the two municipal universities of Akron and Toledo in 1967 became state universities; the University of Cincinnati in 1967 became a state-related university enjoying substantial state government subsidy. In 1964 Cleveland State University was created by law in order to absorb a private institution, Fenn College. In 1965 legislation was enacted that provided for the creation of a state university in 1967 in Dayton known as Wright State University; this new state university grew out of branch programs operated by both Miami University and Ohio State University. And, also in 1967, Youngstown State University became a successor institution to a private university in that city. By 1967, in effect, Ohio had six new state universities alongside the six that had existed in 1964.

At the same time, substantial effort was being made to build university branch campuses, community colleges, and technical colleges as two-year institutions. By 1972 there were four community colleges, eighteen technical colleges, and twenty-four university branch campuses. It might have been desirable to have developed a single structure of two-year campuses in Ohio, but, as I noted earlier, in 1961 the General Assembly had passed legislation permitting all three kinds of institutions. When the Board of Regents was created in 1963, it was faced with the reality of this legislation. Rather than seek to persuade the General Assembly to repeal these laws and to enact legislation for an integrated structure of two-year campuses, the Board of Regents took the position that local communities should exercise their own preference. The Board merely endeavored to prevent a duplication of facilities offering the same instructional programs in the same service area.

In Table 2, I have shown the course of enrollment growth for the various major segments of the public system of higher education over a twenty-year period. It is especially useful to observe the trend in enrollments between 1960 and 1970. In this decade the original six state universities in Ohio increased their enrollment from just under 58,000 students to just under 117,000, or an increase of 100 percent. The new state universities, which were the three municipal universities in 1960, grew from an enrollment of 29,000 to an enrollment of 102,000 students, an increase of 250 percent. The university branches advanced from an enrollment of 9,000 students to an enrollment of more than 27,000 students, an increase of 200 percent. There was no community college enrollment as of 1960, but the four community colleges of 1970 enrolled 26,000 students. And the technical colleges, which did not exist as such in 1960, had an enrollment of 7,000 students in 1970.

Moreover, it is noteworthy that while all the state universities and their branches lost some enrollment in 1972 compared with 1971, the community colleges and technical colleges were continuing to gain students.

TABLE 2

STUDENT ENROLLMENT
AUTUMN HEAD COUNT
OHIO'S PUBLIC COLLEGES AND UNIVERSITIES
1953–1972

	Six State Universities	New State Universities	University Branches	Community Colleges	Technical Colleges
1953	38,179	21,028	3,889		
1954	40,246	22,431	4,552		
1955	44,013	24,203	4,467		
1956	46,849	25,517	6,332		
1957	47,846	26,057	8,070		
1958	51,705	26,722	7,187		
1959	54,449	27,323	8,301		
1960	57,543	29,073	9,361		
1961	62,281	31,941	10,851		
1962	67,346	34,720	13,091		
1963	72,571	37,619	15,253	3,039	
1964	81,812	40,401	18,748	7,446	
1965	88,471	55,796	18,238	11,427	
1966	94,698	59,588	18,053	15,220	
1967	100,018	80,494	20,830	19,098	1,380
1968	106,816	86,262	22,893	22,482	2,054
1969	113,385	97,055	25,966	23,903	5,223
1970	116,832	101,986	27,586	25,947	7,009
1971	116,966	105,440	27,675	30,242	10,214
1972	114,106	106,551	24,923	34,514	12,844

Source: Ohio Board of Regents, *Basic Data Series,* 1973, pp. 11–12.

It is difficult to convey an adequate understanding of all the effort and of all the argument that accompanied this enrollment expansion. I would emphasize here two aspects of this experience. One aspect is that this enrollment growth was made possible only by extensive cooperation between many persons and groups, culminating in action by the chief executive and legislature of Ohio. The other aspect is that this enrollment growth depended heavily upon the expansion of physical facilities that the State of Ohio provided through its program of capital plant financing.

As I look back upon this experience, I am disposed to say that the effort was a success in at least one particular respect. I think it may be fairly said that no student in Ohio who presented himself or herself for enrollment was denied access to higher education in the 1960s. Perhaps there were potential and interested students who were unable to meet the personal cost of higher education. But apart from the constraint of cost, Ohio public higher education did meet the challenge of enrollment expansion during the decade of the 1960s.

To be sure, not every student was always able to enroll in the state university of his or her choice. There were five state universities located in small communities: Ohio University, Miami, Bowling Green, Kent, and Central State. In 1969 the General Assembly by law fixed enrollment ceilings of 20,000 students for Ohio University and Kent, and a ceiling of 15,000 students for Miami and Bowling Green. The enrollment growth of Central State was a disappointment. The Board of Regents recommended these ceilings for two reasons. The communities where these state universities were located were hard pressed to provide the service and other needs of a constantly growing student body. In 1971 Governor Gilligan was disposed to respond to the plea of these communities for state subsidy of the local police and protection services arising from the presence of the state universities. The second reason was a desire to encourage enrollment at the two-year campuses, at the state universities in big cities, and at private colleges and universities. The Board recognized that many students were as much interested in enrolling in higher education to get away from home and parental authority as they were interested in intellectual pursuit, and the Board wrestled with the issue of how far the State of Ohio was obligated to go in accommodating this motivation.

The problem of enrollment expansion at Ohio State was a troublesome and perplexing issue. In 1960 Ohio State had an enrollment of 24,000 students. By 1970 this number had grown to 46,000 students. The 1969 law fixed a limit of 40,000 enrollment for the central campus of Ohio State. The problem was simply the extent to which Ohio State was to be considered a resource for the whole state and the extent to which it was to be considered a resource for the Columbus metropolitan area. It might have been justifiable to build two state universities in Columbus: one to serve all Ohio in its professional and graduate programs and one to serve Columbus in its general undergraduate programs. To some extent this possibility was realized by the development of a University College on a new campus. The original concept was that this University College would be a campus for commuting students residing in the Columbus area. But apparently there were conflicts within Ohio State between the administration which was somewhat Columbus oriented and faculty groups which were not Columbus oriented. Some faculty members were opposed to any action that seemed to cast Ohio State in the role of catering to Columbus residents. As a result, we were never able to achieve a clear-cut and definite local service purpose for the University College of Ohio State.

For this reason, the Board of Regents encouraged the development of a technical college in Columbus in order to make technical education programs available to young people and others residing in the Columbus area. I proposed to the administrative officers and board of trustees at Ohio State that the University make some kind of definite commitment either in terms of metropolitan service or state service, but no such distinction was achieved during my period as chancellor. We did not resolve the issue of the relationship of a "flagship" university in a state system to the metropolitan community in which it happened to be located.

By 1972 the state system of higher education in Ohio began to reach a limit to its enrollment growth, except in the technical education programs. The problem of access to public institutions of higher education had begun to shift to the problem of the kinds of instructional programs appropriate to a "mass" enrollment. I found in general that faculties in public universities were not disposed to worry especially about this new issue. We expanded enrollments in the 1960s but we did not expand equally our concept of higher education purpose and program relevant to the enlarged student population.

Program Expansion

The original statute creating the Ohio Board of Regents provided that no new instructional programs were to be undertaken by any state-assisted college or university without the prior approval of the Board. Although the law gave no definition of a new degree program, the Board assumed that the requirement referred to an entire curriculum leading to the award of a degree. The Board was not concerned with the approval of new courses in an existing degree program, or with changing requirements for award of a degree. The Board limited its jurisdiction to those new instructional endeavors that could be identified as leading to a degree in a field of study not previously offered by a public college or university.

In the course of my eight years of service as chancellor, the Board encountered three major program issues: technical education, doctoral degree education, and medical education. The problem for the Board of Regents in the field of technical education was how to encourage and expand this instructional activity. The problem for the Board in the field of doctoral degree education was how to discourage and restrict this instructional activity. And the problem for the Board in the field of medical education was how much expansion to strive for, what kind of expansion to strive for, and how to meet the costs of expansion.

Over the years, there were a variety of other degree programs demanding the Board's attention, but in general these were not troublesome. All the state universities decided to shift the degree designation for legal education from that of Bachelor of Laws to that of *Juris Doctor*. There was no reason for the Board of Regents not to approve this change. There were other similar kinds of adjustment, including some disposition to change the degree structure in those professional baccalaureate programs having a five-year duration. As an aftermath of the student disorders of 1968, several state universities decided to introduce a new degree program, Bachelor of General Studies or Bachelor of Arts in General Studies, with a wider range of elective course options than had characterized the more traditional programs for a Bachelor of Arts degree. Although having some doubts about the program coherence of this new degree program, again the Board saw no reason to offer any obstacle to the educational change.

Perhaps a word should be said here about the point of view involved in the exercise of this authority of program approval. As the Board of Regents interpreted its role, its concern with the approval of new degree programs was essentially threefold: (1) was there a reasonably evident need for the program; (2) would the program be an unnecessary or expensive duplication of an existing program offered by another public college or university; and (3) would the program have the necessary financial support, either from an adjustment in current resources or from the reasonable prospect of increased appropriations in the next biennium. The Board of Regents did not see its role to be that of determining the minimum desirable standard of quality to be realized in a new degree program. The Board took the position that accrediting agencies should determine the quality of a new degree program, and so the Board gave approval to new degree programs with the condition that they must obtain appropriate accreditation.

The standard of unnecessary or expensive duplication in instructional programs did not give the Board much trouble in interpretation, but it seemed to be a difficult concept to explain to others. Unnecessary duplication meant primarily a duplication of program offerings in the same geographical area, while expensive duplication meant two or more offerings of a program requiring highly specialized facilities and personnel with a very limited student enrollment. Agricultural education, nuclear physics, and a doctoral program in Slavonic languages may be cited as examples of potentially expensive duplication. The Board sought to prevent unnecessary and expensive duplication of instructional programs.

At the time when the Board of Regents was established in 1963, technical education at the associate degree level was not a recognized program in any of the public universities, and was just beginning to be offered by the two newly established community colleges in Ohio. In fact, technical education had been largely ignored in Ohio except by certain proprietary schools and two or three private, nonprofit junior colleges. Then Title VIII of the National Defense Education Act of 1958 had provided federal money to the states to expand both vocational and technical education. This encouragement was strengthened by the enactment of the Vocational Education Act of 1963. In Ohio this federal legislation was administered by the State Board of Education.

When I became chancellor for the Ohio Board of Regents in 1964, I found that the State Board of Education had authorized some ten or twelve technical institutes to operate in conjunction with vocational high schools in various parts of Ohio. None of these technical institutes had been organized under the state technical institute law of 1961. The funding of these technical institutes was being provided entirely by federal grants and by contributed services and costs from school districts. One of these technical institutes as of 1964 was in process of becoming Lorain County Community College. The Cuyahoga Community College, which began instruction in 1963 in many different temporary quarters, expected to offer technical education as soon as it could find the facilities to do so.

At their request, I met in the spring of 1964 with the directors of these technical institutes authorized by the State Board of Education. These men told me that enrollments in technical education were disappointing. They said that the reasons were twofold. Technical education as then organized and operated was too closely identified with high school. And technical education needed new and adequate facilities and other support from state government. The directors wanted to know if I would assist the development of technical education as an integral part of higher education in Ohio. Although I knew very little about technical education as such, I was disposed to be supportive. In the due course of events, I hope it may be fairly said that I became a major force in the development of technical education in Ohio.

There is not space here for me to tell the whole story about the effort to organize and promote technical education as an important, vital part of Ohio higher education. I can do no more than mention certain parts of a fascinating, lengthy struggle. One need was clearly to differentiate technical education from vocational education. It seemed to me that the distinction was clear both in terms of content and prerequisite. Vocational education was a part of secondary education and was concerned to develop trade skills. Technical education followed after secondary education and was concerned to develop knowledge and skills appropriate to para-professional practice. Eventually, this distinction was written into Ohio law with the cooperation of the Superintendent of Public Instruction. Unfortunately, the distinction is not recognized in the administrative organization and funding practice of the federal government up to the present time.

Technical education was developed in Ohio apart from its vocational education counterpart in several ways. Organizationally, technical education programs were offered by technical institutes formed under the Ohio statute of 1961, by community colleges formed under another 1961 statute, by university branches, and even in some instances by state universities. When certain state university faculties were unwilling to authorize the offering of technical education at university branches, I tried to encourage technical institutes to build their facilities alongside the branches. I was surprised to encounter hostility on the part of some university faculties toward technical education. These faculty members considered technical education to be an undesirable part of higher education, and were strongly opposed to my efforts to advance these programs.

Between 1964 and 1972 enrollment in technical education programs increased from around 2,000 students to some 50,000 students. Of these 50,000 students, nearly 20,000 were to be found in community colleges, nearly 13,000 in technical institutes, around 7,000 in university branches, and 10,000 on state university campuses (primarily in Akron, Cincinnati, Toledo, and Youngstown). I considered the development of technical education one of the important accomplishments of state government planning for higher education in Ohio. The same kind of development would not have been possible, I am confident, under the auspices of the Inter-University Council.

A very different kind of story is that involving doctoral degree programs. As I have mentioned earlier, conflict about the expansion of doctoral degree programs was a major factor in the deterioration of cooperative relationships among the state universities prior to 1963. For a long time, indeed from around 1906 to 1956, it was generally recognized that among the state universities of Ohio, only The Ohio State University would develop doctoral degree programs and award doctoral degrees. Then, beginning in 1956, this consensus disappeared. Among the other state universities, Ohio University was the most aggressive in the determination to introduce doctoral degree programs, closely followed by Kent State University. Bowling Green State University was also eager to offer doctoral degrees, although in a more limited number of fields. Miami University under my leadership was the least interested in doctoral degree programs, and among the state university presidents, I was the only one who had served exclusively on the graduate faculty of a major university.

I was somewhat at a loss to understand this great desire to become involved in doctoral programs. It seemed to me that good undergraduate instruction remained a continuing challenge, that graduate education at the Master's degree level was sufficient excursion into post-baccalaureate instruction, and for reasons of economy and quality, doctoral degree education should be left to a few universities throughout the country including Ohio State. I must say that these beliefs were not shared by my presidential colleagues in the other state universities. I gathered that they were convinced, especially after the federal government's enactment of the National Defense Education Act of 1958, that the way to prestige, status, and increased income was the pursuit of doctoral education.

When I became chancellor of the Ohio Board of Regents in 1964, and was faced with the need to complete a Master Plan for Ohio higher education, I immediately confronted the expansion of graduate education at the doctoral level as a major problem. To be sure, as of 1963 when the Board was created, doctoral degree programs were in existence at Ohio University, Kent, and Bowling Green. The Board had no authority to direct the discontinuance of any of these programs. The Board's only authority was to approve or to disapprove additional doctoral degree programs. The Master Plan had to set forth a position on this issue.

As the preparation of this plan proceeded during 1964 and 1965, I quickly learned that the Board of Regents faced two divergent positions on this issue. I met on one occasion with the then academic vice-president and the various deans of the Ohio State University and listened to their vigorous declaration that only Ohio State was qualified by experience, facilities, and distinction of faculty to offer the doctoral degree. I was urged to recommend to the Board of Regents that no new doctoral degree programs should be approved at any other state universities, and it was suggested that the Board ought to find ways to discourage the doctoral degree programs that had been started at Ohio University and elsewhere.

On the other hand, the so-called "emerging" universities insisted that they were entitled to develop doctoral degree programs. They resented any insinuation that their faculties were inferior to the faculty of Ohio State, or of emerging universities in other states. They argued that they could not recruit new faculty talent from the leading universities unless they promised to develop doctoral programs. They pointed out that federal government funds were available for new doctoral degree programs and for an increasing volume of science research. And although the point was not emphasized, I became aware that graduate education was an important factor in meeting the staffing needs for undergraduate instruction in a period of expanding enrollment. In fact, the costs of undergraduate education were substantially reduced by the employment of teaching assistants, especially the costs of lower division education.

In issuing its draft master plan in 1965, the Board of Regents set the strengthening and expansion of graduate study at the doctoral level as a major objective of state policy. The Board pledged this effort primarily at Ohio State and the University of Cincinnati, but opened the door to further doctoral programs at other state-assisted universities "in response to special circumstances and needs." But none of us was able to explain what these special circumstances and needs might be. The Board simply pledged itself to careful coordination of this expansion.

In practice, in 1965 and thereafter, the Board of Regents approved new doctoral degree programs in quite limited numbers, and mostly in the general fields of the humanities, social sciences, biological sciences, and physical sciences. The one professional field of expansion was in teacher education. I find from the record that forty new doctoral degree programs were approved by the Board of Regents between 1964 and 1972, all but two of these at the seven emerging state universities.

In 1970 when the danger of an oversupply of doctoral degree recipients suddenly became apparent, the Board of Regents declared a moratorium on the consideration of further doctoral programs. During the calendar year 1970 the Board was engaged in the preparation of its second Master Plan, which was duly published in January, 1971. Personally, I take great pride in this Master Plan; it represents what I think a state master plan ought to provide. In referring to instruction at the doctoral level the Board made a distinction between programs in the arts and sciences and programs in professional education. The Board set forth data about current output of doctoral students and then established objectives for enrollment and degrees to be awarded by 1980. The Board proposed a distribution of effort among the nine state universities approved to award the doctor's degree.

This distribution of effort was confirmed by a policy

statement adopted by the Board of Regents on June 16, 1972, a statement agreed to by all the state universities. Ohio State and Cincinnati were recognized as the leading research universities offering an extensive scope of doctoral degree programs, with a heavy emphasis upon research competence. Bowling Green State University, Kent State University, Miami University, and Ohio University were expected to emphasize the education of graduate students primarily for careers as undergraduate instructors in four-year colleges. The public universities in major urban areas were asked to concentrate their development of doctoral programs in professional fields for persons already employed in their area and desiring improved professional competence. I consider this 1972 agreement a major planning accomplishment and as rational a distribution of effort as possible.

Medical Education

No program problem confronting the Ohio Board of Regents during the years 1964 to 1972 was more troublesome or more complicated than that of medical education. I have mentioned earlier the directive of the Ohio General Assembly in 1959 to the Interim Commission on Education Beyond the High School to make a study of medical education in the state. The report of the consultant for this study was released early in 1962. The Interim Commission itself on December 28, 1962, recommended the creation of a new medical college in Toledo.

In 1964 the Board of Regents through its master plan study undertook to review the issue further. Obviously, the first step was to begin a new medical college in Toledo. House Bill No. 7 was passed at a special session of the Ohio General Assembly on December 17, 1964, and approved by Governor Rhodes on the next day; it established the Medical College of Ohio at Toledo. The State of Ohio was now launched upon the effort to build a new college of medicine. In its 1966 Master Plan the Board of Regents pledged its efforts to expedite the development of the new college, and promised in the near future to determine whether or not there was a need for another college of medicine.

I cannot undertake here to tell the story of the various frustrations encountered in the development of the Medical College of Ohio at Toledo. I shall mention only the major issues as I saw them. Medical educators in the United States appear to be committed to the idea of a health science center that brings together in one place education for the doctor of medicine degree, internship and residency training, health research, education for health research, patient care, education in the health-related professions, and continuing education in the health professions. In this health science center, the emphasis is upon the expansion of knowledge in the health sciences rather than upon the education of doctors and other personnel to provide health care to patients. And I may add that the health science center is a costly set of facilities to build and an even costlier set of activities to operate.

I had the obviously misguided idea that the new medical college in Toledo could be developed according to a somewhat different concept. I hoped that the new college would emphasize the education of doctors for patient care, and that the medical instruction could be provided through the cooperation of existing patient care facilities in Toledo. But medical educators were convinced that only a large and expensive health science center could meet the needs of modern medical education, and that this health science center must bring together people committed to health science research and to health science education. Doctors engaged primarily in patient care, I was told, were not qualified to be medical educators.

With the decline of federal government funding of new health science centers, the burden of the cost of developing this Toledo health science center fell entirely upon the State of Ohio. Local community support, so lavishly promised in 1962, was not forthcoming in 1966. By 1971 the State of Ohio had appropriated over 40 million dollars for capital facilities at the Toledo Medical College, and eventually as much as 100 million dollars would probably be required. Operating appropriations in 1972–73 came to 5 million dollars for medical education and 3 million dollars for hospital care. And the total number of medical students in the autumn of 1972 was just 133.

In its 1971 Master Plan, the Board of Regents asserted that there was a need to educate more doctors in Ohio. Expansions then planned were designed to admit 705 students a year, and the Board upon the advice of a medical consultant declared that the objective by 1980 should be 1000 entering students a year. The problem was whether or not the four existing medical schools, including that of Case Western Reserve, should be expanded from 700 to 1000 students per class. The alternative was to develop two new medical colleges, one in the Dayton area and one in the Akron area, with an entering class of 150 each.

When I left in 1972 this issue was not yet resolved. But personally I was convinced that the Board of Regents would never be able to persuade the existing health science centers to give new attention to the education of doctors primarily to engage in the delivery of health care and to involve various community hospitals in this endeavor. Accordingly, I personally was convinced that two new medical colleges were desirable. I wish I knew how to guarantee that they would develop differently from the current concept of a health science center.

The Impact Upon Private Higher Education

There were other planning issues that I might discuss here, but there is one failure that does require mention. In the 1966 Master Plan, the Board of Regents acknowledged the existence of the many colleges and universities operating under private sponsorship in Ohio and declared that public policy should seek to strengthen and assist them "in appropriate ways." The Board pledged itself in expanding public higher education to try to minimize unfavorable repercussions upon these private institutions. The Board advocated a scheme of tuition equalization grants for Ohio residents enrolled in private colleges and proposed for study an arrangement to assist private institutions in building new facilities.

In 1968 the Ohio General Assembly did enact legislation recommended by the Board of Regents creating a higher educational facility commission to build and lease educational facilities for private colleges and universities. The advantage in this arrangement was to make it possible for private institutions to borrow capital plant funds at lower interest rates, even as the public institutions did. The revenue bonds sold by the commission were held to be bonds of a state government agency, and the interest income was therefore exempt from federal income taxation. This new arrangement was utilized only on a limited scale by private colleges and universities, since there were issues of constitutionality affecting the church-related colleges to be resolved.

In 1969 the Ohio Board of Regents sponsored legislation enacted by the General Assembly establishing an Ohio instructional grant program based upon student financial need. The grant schedule was twice as large for students in private higher education as for students in public higher education. Thus the equalization principle was incorporated into this legislation. The Board of Regents was advised informally by legal consultants that a grant to students not based on financial need would be unconstitutional.

But the major impact of public higher education upon private higher education was not anticipated by the Ohio Board of Regents and did not become clearly evident until

1969 and 1970. As public facilities for higher education were expanded, especially in urban communities, enrollments in private colleges and universities began to decline. This decline was especially evident in the cities that had not previously had public institutions of higher education. This enrollment decline began in 1969 and had become noticeable indeed by 1972.

Before 1969 the Board of Regents had cooperated in the sponsorship of legislation and other arrangements that resulted in the transformation of three private colleges into two state universities and one community college. In 1969 the Board of Regents assisted in the preparation of legislation that made possible state government financial assistance to the medical school of Case Western Reserve University. The chairman of the University Board of Trustees informed me and the members of the Board of Regents that the university could no longer meet the operating costs of the medical school. I was instrumental in presenting their plight to the Governor and to legislative leaders. The consequence was the beginning of state financial support to Case Western Reserve University for medical education. I was convinced that this assistance was much cheaper for Ohio than building a new medical school in Cleveland, or taking over the complete financial support of the school.

As new facilities for public higher education became available, the tuition differential in the charges to students between public and private institutions became a positive economic incentive encouraging students to enroll in the public institutions. I simply had not foreseen this event. The issue then was what to do about it.

When the Board turned to preparation of a new Master Plan in 1970, the presidents of private colleges and universities were greatly concerned about their financial future. They proposed to the Board that the State of Ohio enter into contracts with their institutions to pay part of the instructional cost for Ohio students enrolling in their institutions. I was sympathetic to this proposal, as were members of the Board. The problem was twofold: how legally and constitutionally to provide this assistance and how to find the state funds to pay for the new arrangement.

Needless to say, the state university presidents were opposed to any subsidy to the private institutions. They were opposed to such a subsidy while state appropriations were on such a scale that increased charges to students in the public institutions were necessary. And they were opposed to such a subsidy unless accompanied by some limitation upon the instructional expenditures of the private institutions. I thought this second concern was a reasonable one, but I was not equally convinced about the need to keep tuition charges at state universities low for all students.

In the 1971 Master Plan the Board of Regents came up with a proposal for a contract arrangement with private colleges and universities. The Board recommended legislation authorizing it to enter into contracts whereby the Board would pay to any private institution for each student enrolled as an upper division student upon completion of the program at a public two-year campus the same instructional subsidy that a public university would have received if the student had enrolled there. In addition, the college or university would have had to agree to charge the student no more than the student would have paid at a state university. Governor Gilligan approved this recommendation of the Board of Regents in his message to the General Assembly on March 15, 1971.

The proposal was not enacted into law, however, primarily because of opposition from the private colleges and universities. They were fearful that the proposal would create new problems for them: a possible further decline in lower division enrollments, a two-priced system of tuition charges at the upper division level that might create conflict among students, and undesirable restrictions upon instructional costs. I thought the experiment was worth trying, but perhaps the private institutions were correct in their fears. In any event, the proposal died and the problem of tuition competition remained.

On the eve of my departure in June, 1972, I put forth another proposal on a personal basis, but no one listens to a lame-duck chancellor. I shall say more about this proposal in the next chapter. But since June, 1972, I have continued to be greatly concerned about this problem of the tuition differential between public and private colleges and universities. In 1973 both the Committee for Economic Development and the Carnegie Commission on Higher Education have spoken to this problem. I, myself, have still another idea on this subject, which I presented at the 1974 annual meeting of the Association of American Colleges. I place this issue at the top of the list for the current agenda of state government planning for higher education.

Conclusion

The essential governmental leadership in the development of higher education policy and program in this country has been exercised by the fifty state governments. The role of the federal government has been essentially more limited in scope and objective. At the undergraduate level the federal government has been primarily concerned with equality of access to higher education, and this objective has been promoted through a variety of student financial assistance programs, including student loans, guaranteed student loans, educational opportunity grants, and work-study grants. I wish that these programs were sufficient in magnitude to underwrite equality of access and to eliminate the need for colleges and universities to spend some of their own general income for student financial assistance.

In addition, the federal government through its research grants has supported the research programs of major research universities and has at the same time assisted the graduate education of students, especially in the biological sciences, physical sciences, engineering, and mathematics. Graduate education and basic research, both major purposes of our research universities, have become possible on an advanced scale in this country only because of federal government financing.

But apart from student financial assistance and the support of research, the federal government has not exercised a major influence upon the conduct of higher education in the United States. Rather it has been our state governments that have had to make the important decisions about the number, location, and enrollment size of public institutions of higher education; about the kinds of instructional programs to be made available to students; about the charges to students for instructional service; about the admission standards and quality of instructional programs; and about the desirable relationship of public higher education to private higher education. In making these kinds of decisions the chief executive and the legislature of a state need professional and practical advice. It was this kind of advice which the Ohio Board of Regents as a state planning agency in the field of higher education tried to provide.

The problems of planning for higher education within our state governments have changed somewhat in the last two years, but the need for planning and for action has not disappeared. There are exciting and challenging years still ahead.

4

State Budgeting for Higher Education:
1964–1972

STATE BUDGETING FOR HIGHER EDUCATION IS CONCERNED with two inter-related objectives. The first objective is to provide the various state-assisted colleges and universities with state tax appropriations and with student fee income adequate to meet their basic operating needs. The second objective is to achieve equity or fairness in the distribution of this available income among the various state-assisted colleges and universities. Unless state budgeting meets these two objectives, it has failed to accomplish its purpose.

Obviously, the state colleges and universities themselves must play a major part in the determination of appropriation needs. Each institution is well aware of the work it does, the work it would like to do, the costs involved, and the income it would like to have. State government officials know what has been appropriated previously in support of higher education activities and institutions, but they are not necessarily conversant with the details of how the institutions themselves manage their income resources. State government officials are dependent upon the financial information provided by the institutions themselves. Close and cooperative relationships are needed between state government officials on the one hand and institutional officials on the other hand.

It may be well to pause here in order to observe one of the unique financial characteristics of state-assisted colleges and universities. This characteristic is that these institutions have multiple sources of income. State governments do not appropriate from state tax sources the total operating income or the total capital income of state-assisted colleges and universities. For example, the public institutions of higher education in Ohio had income amounting to approximately 850 million dollars in the fiscal year ending June 30, 1973. Of this income the State of Ohio provided 285 million dollars, or 33.5 percent. Other income is derived from charges to students, federal government grants, endowment, gifts, sales, and miscellaneous sources.

Because state-assisted colleges and universities obtain only part of their total income from state government, I insisted, as chancellor of the Ohio Board of Regents, upon two budgetary concepts. Each college and university created under state law should have the status of a government corporation, of a "body politic and corporate," and I was successful in getting this concept enacted into law. In addition, I argued that the state appropriation was in effect a subsidy to the operation of a government created corporation. And I was successful in persuading the State Department of Finance and the Ohio General Assembly to adopt this appropriation practice. I considered both of these arrangements essential to a satisfactory state budget process.

In returning to my concern with the budget process as such, I need to emphasize the matter of the respective roles of a state board of higher education and a state department of finance, or a state budget office, in preparing the appropriation recommendations of an executive budget. The 1963 statute creating the Board of Regents specified that the Board should review the appropriation requests of the public community colleges and the state colleges and universities and should submit to the department of finance and to the chairmen of the house and senate finance committees its recommendations in regard to the biennial higher education appropriation of the state. In conferring this authority upon the Board of Regents the statute further directed that the board should work "in close cooperation" with the director of finance in preparing its recommendations and in "all other matters" concerning the expenditure of appropriated funds by the state-assisted colleges and universities.

I interpreted this language to mean two things. I considered the Board of Regents to be the state budget agency for higher education. At the same time, I felt that the Board had to keep the Director of Finance fully informed at all stages of the budget process. The Director of Finance—there were two of them during the period of the Rhodes Administration—concurred in my interpretation. The staff of the Department of Finance specializing in the review of higher education budgets was transferred to the Board of Regents. At the same time, I saw to it that I conferred frequently with the Director of Finance about the higher education budget. Mr. Howard L. Collier as Deputy Director of Finance and subsequently as Director of Finance under Governor Rhodes was most cooperative and supportive at all times. I must make the same comment about Dr. Harold Hovey, Director of Finance during the first two years under Governor Gilligan.

I think it is imperative that a state board of higher education have a major role in the state appropriation process. Otherwise the state board has very little utility. The appropriation process is the primary influence that a state government has in the continuing relationship between state government and higher education. If the state board of higher education is removed from this process, it is denied its major opportunity to influence state higher education policy. Moreover, if the state board does not have this role, then the job of budget review and recommendation must and does fall upon the budget staff of the Governor. I always endeavored to make sure that the Board of Regents performed its budget work in such a fashion that the De-

partment of Finance and the Governor could have confidence in the data presented to them and at the same time
have the opportunity to indicate desirable policy ideas of
their own.

During my years as chancellor in Ohio, there was not an
official agent of the General Assembly designated as the
legislative budget officer. The director of the Legislative
Service Commission provided staff assistance to the two
finance committees, but generally this staff assistance was
concerned with details of the appropriation measure rather
than with issues of substance. In 1971 with a Democratic
Governor and a Republican legislature, the Speaker of the
House and the President pro tem of the Senate did desig-
nate a special staff officer to watch over the appropriation-
taxation process. For all practical purposes this individual
did serve as a legislative budget officer. I can only add that
he was also a very helpful person insofar as the higher
education appropriation was concerned.

In the spirit of the language of the law as I understood it,
I endeavored to work closely with the chairmen of the two
finance committees, one in the House of Representatives
and one in the Senate. In addition, as I quickly learned,
there were certain key members of both committees who
were disposed to be helpful, who kept me informed of
various developments, and who were inclined to support
the case for higher education appropriations. And there
were always persons who could be counted upon to be
unfriendly. I found that higher education had legislative
friends who were Republicans and legislative friends who
were Democrats. I also found that higher education had
legislative enemies, some of whom were Republicans and
some of whom were Democrats. For some reason, I seem to
remember more non-friends among Republicans than
Democrats; I guess I expected more from the Republicans!

I would emphasize that the formal appropriation hearings before the finance committees of the legislature were
an important, but only a small, part of the appropriation

process. The hearings set the stage for later committee deliberation; the impression made by higher education spokesmen in these hearings could and did influence subsequent decisions. But it was in the executive sessions of the finance committees, in the informal discussions among committee members, and in the interaction of committee members with the legislative leaders that the final verdict about appropriation amounts was eventually made. To the extent that I was able to participate in this informal process, I was an effective representative of the needs of the State of Ohio in higher education.

Higher Education Expenditures and Income

At an early stage in my development of budget procedure for the Ohio Board of Regents, I was confronted with the need to define just what expenditures and what income the state budget and appropriation process were concerned with. I had given a great deal of thought to this question as president of Miami University. I found no reason to alter my thinking on this score when I became chancellor.

For a long time in the budgeting and financial reporting of colleges and universities, it had been customary to divide the activities and programs of colleges and universities into three major categories: educational and general, auxiliary enterprises, and student aid. As a state university president, I became convinced that a fivefold classification was essential, and as chancellor I was able to influence the practice of public institutions in Ohio so that this expanded classification was adopted. It divided programs into five categories: instruction and general, research, public service, auxiliary services, and student aid.

Perhaps a word about budgeting and accounting is justified here. Under Ohio law, the Auditor of State had the authority to prescribe accounting practices for state government agencies, presumably including state-assisted colleges and universities. I suggested to the Auditor of State in 1965 that some agreement about accounting practices was necessary between my office and his in order to perform the budget task of the Board of Regents effectively. The Auditor of State at that time was a Republican friend, Roger Cloud, the former Speaker of the Ohio House of Representatives. Mr. Cloud agreed to retain a consultant to develop a uniform chart of accounts for state higher education institutions, the consultant was appointed after discussion with me, and the consultant developed a chart of accounts to meet the mutual interests of the Auditor and of the Board of Regents. The state universities were fully involved in the development. The Auditor of State then officially prescribed this chart of accounts.

Under the fivefold classification of institutional activities, I was able to point out that the State of Ohio was primarily concerned with the adequacy and equity of the support provided for instruction. The only research interest of the State was in the support of the agricultural experiment station. Initially, the State of Ohio had just two major concerns with public service: the agricultural extension service and the subsidy of teaching hospitals. The State of Ohio was not involved in support of any auxiliary services, and as of 1964 it was not involved in support of student aid.

If the State of Ohio therefore was primarily concerned with support of instructional expenditures, then an important additional policy issue immediately arose. What income should the State of Ohio review in determining the level of needed support for instructional programs? It seemed to me that only two sources of instructional income were important to the State as a state: state appropriations and instructional charges to students. I was aware that state universities might have endowment income and gift income available for instructional expenses. Some federal government grants might also be available under the Morrill Act of 1890, under the National Defense Act of 1958, and as overhead on government contracts. I was opposed to any effort to deduct this other income from state appropriations and from student charges. It was not the role of the State to ensure an absolute equality in instructional resources, but to ensure a relative equality in what the State provided. Certainly state institutions should be given a positive incentive to obtain other available income, and not provided with a positive discouragement to this effort.

Another policy issue was that of the desirable distribution of instructional support between state appropriations and charges to students. I was disposed to answer this question on a pragmatic basis. There was an existing level of student instructional charges in existence as of 1964. As we approached the 1965–67 biennium we should project as limited an increase as possible. Actually student instructional charges for three quarters or two semesters as of 1964–65 varied from $375 to $450. The objective from 1965–67 was to maintain this level, although some increases were made by the institutions during the biennium.

By the biennium 1967–69 it was clear that the budget process of state government in support of instruction would have to be concerned with charges to students as well as with appropriations from the general revenue fund. The decision to impose restrictions upon the state universities, insofar as instructional charges were concerned, arose during the appropriation hearings in 1967. The house finance committee wanted assurance from the state university presidents that they would not increase charges to students beyond the guidelines recommended by the Board of Regents. When these assurances were not forthcoming on a basis satisfactory to the committee members, the finance committee wrote into the appropriation law a provision giving the Board of Regents control over student fee charges.

Actually, the distribution of the costs of instruction between state appropriations and charges to students is a major policy issue, and it should be resolved during the appropriation process. There are some states where some kind of formula is employed in this distribution, such as that student tuition shall be one-quarter or one-third of the average cost of undergraduate instruction. In 1973 there were two national studies which suggested that student tuition charges in state universities should be increased to the point where they would approximate about 50 percent of the average cost of undergraduate instruction. Whatever the formula or whatever the practice, the distribution of income for instruction between state tax support and charges to students is a political decision and ought to be made, I believe, through the political process. This is not a decision to be left to the judgment of boards of trustees or of faculties of state universities. It is a decision to be made by governors and legislators.

Charges to Students

At this point it is appropriate to add certain additional comments about this difficult policy issue involving the pricing of higher education instructional service to students. When publicly sponsored higher education began in Ohio in 1804 and 1809, the income for the operation and capital plant of both Ohio University and Miami University was expected to come entirely from the land grant to each university and from charges to students. Only in the 1880s did the State of Ohio begin to appropriate general fund revenue for the support of these two universities and the new state university established in 1870, Ohio State. I assume that other states have had a somewhat similar history. In any event, charges to students were an important source of income to so-called state universities prior to the Civil War.

The federal government's Morrill Act of 1862 is usually considered to have begun the tradition in the United States that state colleges and universities should have low tuition charges to students. If higher education opportunity was to be opened increasingly to youth of the artisan and mechanic classes, then it was said that tuition charges would have to remain modest. In any event, as state-sponsored higher education began to expand, particularly after 1900, tuition charges were kept low. I ought to note here also that tuition costs at private colleges were not especially high in these earlier days. When I entered college in 1929, the tuition charge at a private church-related college was $100 a semester. At a public university that year I would have paid an instructional fee of around $35. When I entered graduate study in 1934 at a leading private university, I paid $200 a semester in tuition. Today, in 1974, the tuition charge at the private college is $1400 a semester, and the charge at the private university is $1700 a semester, while the instructional charge at a public university in my home state of Indiana is $350 a semester.

In any event, public higher education in this country endeavors to maintain low tuition charges, and there is a good deal of debate about whether or not this maintenance of low tuition is a realistic and even desirable public policy. I cannot discuss this policy issue in all its ramifications here. On the one hand, it is argued that many students in state universities come from upper income families, and could well afford to pay more for their education. On the other hand, it is argued that many students in state universities come from middle income families, and that these families would be hard pressed to meet higher tuition charges. It is also argued that subsidy of students based upon family income would be more equitable than subsidy of state universities in order to maintain low charges for all students.

In any event, I wish here to mention certain specific questions encountered in Ohio in 1969 and 1971. In 1969 Governor Rhodes was reluctant to recommend a further tax increase after one in 1967, and so the matter of increases in student charges came up once again. I proposed a general increase in student charges, which would have advanced the charges per quarter from around $170 to $250 at the undergraduate level, and from $170 to $300 at the graduate level. At the same time, the Board of Regents made it very clear that it was recommending these increases only with the understanding that the State would adopt a student aid program. By adopting a program of financial assistance to undergraduate students, the State could make certain that none of the increase would be paid by students from families below the median family income in Ohio. The Governor proposed a new base for the sales tax, a gross receipts tax, which would have produced more income for the general revenue fund and which would have made these tuition increases unnecessary. But there was a good deal of opposition to this proposal from retail merchants and from service businesses, and the recommendation was not enacted.

Students on various state university campuses were quite vocal in 1969 in their opposition to any increase in student charges. This opposition was understandable, but not very well informed. Student leaders ignored the issue of whether or not the state universities needed more income, and paid little attention to the alternative choices for obtaining more income. They said nothing about the proposed student aid program, which led me to believe that most, if not all, of these leaders came from families above the median family income. The students simply insisted that they wanted no increase in charges. It should also be noted that in 1969 student activism was quite prevalent on various campuses; there had been several occasions of campus disorder in Ohio in 1968. It appeared that the issue of charges to students might become a major campus issue in 1969.

Governor Rhodes indicated to me in the course of a discussion soon after his 1969 budget message that he would like to compromise this fee issue in some way. Eventually, the decision was made to reduce the state subsidy for out-of-state undergraduate students. This decision meant a substantial increase in the charges to out-of-state students and a modest increase in tuition charges to students living in Ohio. The subsidy for out-of-state students was reduced to one-half, with the prospect of eliminating the entire subsidy in the next biennium. The principal consequence I could see, as a result of the student opposition to our original proposals, was to increase the costs for out-of-state students and to reduce consequently the number of these students. I assume this result was desired by those who made the final decision.

In 1971 a different kind of issue arose. Elected in November, 1970, Governor Gilligan went to work immediately after his inauguration in January, 1971, to prepare his proposals for a state income tax and for a considerable upgrading in state services through increased expenditures. In our discussions about the higher education budget, I learned that Governor Gilligan was interested in how the "Yale Plan" of income-contingent loans to students could be applied to public higher education. I tried to suggest that the circumstances of public higher education were different from those of private higher education, and that the concept of income-contingent loans needed careful consideration before it could be applied to the state universities in Ohio. To my dismay, I learned that Governor Gilligan was interested in developing a proposal that would have required every student to enter into an income-contingent loan for the entire amount of the state subsidy for his or her instruction. I was opposed to this proposal for both practical and philosophical reasons. In practical terms, it seemed to me that the income-contingent loan proposal would be misleading to many at a time when the State was seeking to adopt an income tax. The plan would produce no immediate income for the state universities, but would produce revenue for the state government only several years away from the present. As a matter of principle, I thought, and still think, that a social investment in higher education as well as an individual investment is desirable. The proposal of Governor Gilligan seemed to imply that the social investment was undesirable or unnecessary.

Later I tried to interest Governor Gilligan in a different idea, in the idea that any future student fee increases at the state universities should be made on the basis of an option to students: an option to pay the increases currently or to pay them later on the basis of future income. This proposal would provide income now to the state universities by means of a state-financed income-contingent loan fund that would accept the student loan documents and pay the institution the face value of the loans. I proposed also that the same income-contingent loans made available to students in the public institutions should be made equally available to students in the private institutions. Governor Gilligan indicated interest in this proposal but it was not pressed in the 1973 legislature.

I should add that in 1971 I did not receive a single communication from any student organization or any student indicating support for or opposition to my position on Governor Gilligan's contingent loan proposal. In 1971 students didn't care what might happen, or did not pay any particular attention to the issue. Legislators indicated to me that they heard very little about the issue in their home communities. The big political battle of 1971 and of 1972 was the new state income tax enacted in December, 1971.

As part of my discussion of the future financing of higher education at the time of my departure from the chancellorship in Ohio, I suggested also the possibility of differential pricing at different places of instruction. I proposed instructional charges of $150 per quarter at public two-year campuses, $300 per quarter for undergraduates in the state universities, and $400 per quarter for graduate students in the state universities. This proposal was intended to do two things: to encourage enrollment in the two-year institutions, and to reduce enrollment pressures at the state universities. I also had in mind that those who are experimenting with their interest in higher education should not be discouraged from doing so by the factor of cost. Those who are more certain of their interests and abilities could afford to pay more, I thought, for their instructional opportunity. More recently, the State University of New York has adopted the practice of differential pricing by level of instruction rather than by place of instruction. I now think this method is a better idea than mine.

Adequate Support

No budget issue in state support of higher education is more troublesome than the question of what constitutes adequate support. I have mentioned this problem in an earlier chapter. I have come to believe that adequacy is an incremental attribute rather than an absolute. I suppose adequacy is related to the idea of progress or betterment. If we as individuals sense that our economic status is improving, even if the improvement is not substantial, we are inclined to self-satisfaction. So it is with higher education institutions as individual enterprises. If there is a sense of financial improvement, then there is a tendency to consider current financial support as adequate.

At one or another time during my period as chancellor, I dreamed of making a quantum advance in the income support of higher education. I learned that university presidents were less interested in big leaps forward than in continuous steps forward. The thrust of higher education budgeting in the 1960s was incremental, not precipitate. And I suspect this same circumstance will prevail during the 1970s. Today, with the rapid advance in price levels of the last two or three years, there is a new incentive toward incremental advance in state support of higher education: we must obviously keep pace with inflation, so the argument goes.

From time to time, I and many others had been inclined to compare Ohio's support of public higher education with that of other states, especially to that of other states in the Middle West. I even introduced such comparisons as a part of the basic statistical data which the Board of Regents published about Ohio higher education. There were several kinds of comparisons that could be made. These included the total appropriations in support of higher education per capita of state population, the proportion of per capita income appropriated for higher education, the proportion of the general fund appropriated for higher education, the total amount of federal government support received by public higher education in each state, the average faculty salaries of comparable state universities, and the total student fees charged by comparable state universities. In general, I found that Ohio did not rank well in these comparisons. For example, in terms of appropriations per capita, Ohio ranked forty-seventh in 1972, the average for all fifty states being state appropriations in the amount of $41.91 per person as opposed to $30.19 in Ohio. In the proportion of per capita income appropriated for higher education, Ohio ranked forty-third in 1972, appropriating only seven-tenths of one percent of per capita income, while the average for all fifty states was 1.1 percent of per capita income. We did usually rank high when it came to instructional charges to students, and it was in this way that Ohio maintained its competitive position in higher education.

To be sure, in terms of total dollars appropriated for higher education, Ohio did not look too bad. But this circumstance was simply a function of size. The sixth largest state in terms of population, Ohio was, after 1967, usually about eighth among the states in total dollars spent for higher education. And when it came to percentage of increase in appropriations over the preceding year or biennium, Ohio was twenty-second in 1965, first in 1967, fifth in 1969, and thirtieth in 1971.

I never did find that these comparisons were of very great help during the appropriation process. They were reassuring to me that the state universities were scarcely being profligate in their requests for appropriations. But to the chief executive and legislature, the comparisons suggested only that Ohio was being properly cautious in its expenditures for higher education. I was never able to tell the Governor or the General Assembly exactly what Ohio was buying with the money spent on higher education. Of course, I had data about student enrollment and degrees awarded. But I was never in a position to say that if Ohio spent one dollar more per capita on higher education, 5 percent more persons in the population would lead happier lives, or that the gross state product would be increased by 3 percent, or that the number of jobs available would be increased by 2 percent. We simply don't know what higher education produces for the money expended, or what the quality of the product may be.

The Budget System for Current Operations

I have mentioned earlier that the Inter-University Council of Ohio, about 1959, had begun a study to determine the costs per student credit hour in various fields of study. The results of these studies were available to me in 1964 as I began to explore how the Board of Regents could best analyze appropriation requests for higher education, and how the Board could best recommend appropriation needs to the Governor and General Assembly. The basic problem obviously centered in instructional costs. As of 1964–65, about 88 percent of the state appropriation in support of higher education went to instructional programs. This proportion was to decline to 77 percent by 1972–73, but this is a later story. Instructional support was the essence of the state budget effort.

Moreover, my years as a state university president convinced me that the essential need was for an equitable distribution of the state instructional appropriation among the various state-assisted colleges and universities. I want to dwell at some length upon this concept of equity, because it is central to my own thinking about state government budgeting for higher education and because it is often misunderstood in writings about public higher education.

By equity, I do not mean that every state college or every state university should receive exactly the same appropriation per student enrolled. I have heard of one or two states where this kind of definition prevails. By equity, I meant that each state-assisted institution should have available to it the same resources in state appropriations and in student fees per full-time equivalent student *enrolled in comparable programs of instruction.* There are differences in instructional programs among colleges and universities, and there are differences in costs among instructional programs. These differences must be accommodated in a state budget process. But in terms of comparable programs, I believed strongly, and still do believe, that each institution should have the same available resources per student.

I know that the larger a college or university, the larger will be the available resources when appropriations are based upon enrollment. And I realize that as enrollment grows, the marginal cost for each additional student will be less than the average cost. In a period of rapid enrollment growth, I saw no reason to be worried about these circumstances.

The usual argument against equal distribution of available resources is that it forces upon state institutions of higher education a pattern of common endeavor, a uniformity of effort, a dull mediocrity. It is claimed that colleges and universities should be different, and that resources should be provided to encourage differences. Now this kind of argument sounds impressive upon the face of it. It is surprising how enthusiastic some higher educationists can become for diversity, for differences, for nonuniformity; and then on other occasions they are equally enthusiastic for equality. My problem as chancellor simply was that no one ever provided me with a rational or objective case for spending less money on some students and more money on other students. Sometimes I was told that bright students deserved more expenditure for their education than average or dull students. Sometimes I was told that students living away from home needed more money spent on their social and recreational needs than students living at home. Perhaps these are factual propositions. I was never convinced, however.

I argued that the average student, or the less than average student, might need more money spent on his or her education than the bright student. I argued that the student living at home might need more social and recreational opportunities than the student living away from home, or that the student living away from home ought to be willing to pay for all the special costs resulting from living in a special environment. Regardless of these arguments, valid or otherwise, the circumstance simply was that I thought it was the essence of ethical administration to treat students in similar instructional programs in the same way regardless of where they might be enrolled. I saw no ethical basis for considering the instructional need of the student in Cleveland State University to be less than the instructional need of the student enrolled at Miami University. And that remains my position today.

To be sure, there are differences among students, there are differences among faculty members, and there are differences among state universities. Moreover, I do not object to these differences. But I think these differences are based upon certain factors not necessarily related to equality of instructional income. And different institutions do have differences in income, arising from the attitudes of alumni and from the efforts made by administrators and others to raise money from non-state government sources. I had no desire to control these differences, and I think no state board of higher education should endeavor to do so.

My concern was that I did not wish ever to be accused of playing favorites among state universities. In my eight years as chancellor in Ohio, I was criticized on numerous occasions for assorted failings. But at least I was never criticized for favoring one university over another, one area of the state over another, one student over another. And I fought as effectively as I knew how to prevent an appropriation process that appeared to reward one university and to punish another, to give preference to one university and to express displeasure with another.

How then does one proceed to accomplish equity in the distribution of the available appropriations for higher education? I decided, and my board members agreed, that the appropriate procedure was to develop models, or a generalized picture, of instructional costs per student by various program categories. These models had to be based upon experience; they had to be related to actual expenditure patterns. Therefore the Board of Regents had to have a uniform information system that provided comparable data about enrollments, staffing, facilities, and financing. Moreover, these models had to be different to reflect differences in staffing patterns, support costs, and instructional outputs among different programs. For example, doctoral programs and medical programs must make allowance for faculty effort devoted to research and public service, because in graduate programs these are important outputs along with the instruction of students. Or, to state the proposition differently, graduate study and graduate professional study involve the advancement of knowledge and the utilization of knowledge as an integral part of instruction. And finally, the models had to be reasonably simple for presentation to the executive and legislative branches of state government.

I shall not endeavor here to review our experience in Ohio with a uniform information system, with a resource analysis system, or with budget models. Needless to say, these were sizeable efforts requiring the fullest cooperation of all state-assisted institutions and the extensive use of electronic data processing procedures. We collected and we analyzed an extensive array of data. We developed our own taxonomy of instructional programs some time before the Higher Education General Information Survey of the federal government developed its own taxonomy, which is now commonly observed in the United States. We recognized and accounted for five levels of instruction: the associate degree or two-year level; the baccalaureate level; the master's degree level; the doctor's degree level; and the graduate professional level. I do not want to suggest that we solved all the instructional or cost problems of higher education by our procedure. I do want to suggest that we did develop a practical and, I believe, equitable basis for approaching the expenditure needs of higher education.

For reasons of convenience and simplicity of presentation, we eventually arrived at an eight category grouping of instructional programs that lent themselves to averaging and to differentiation on a comparable basis. These eight program categories were designated as follows:

1. *General Studies Programs* (lower division, general education in the arts and sciences)

2. *Technical Education Programs* (Two-year technologies)

3. *Baccalaureate General Programs* (undergraduate instruction in the arts and sciences, teacher education, and business administration)

4. *Baccalaureate Professional Programs* (undergraduate instruction in agriculture, allied health professions, architecture, art, engineering, home economics, music, pharmacy, social work, technology, and theater)

5. *Master's Degree Programs*

6. *Graduate Professional Programs* (dentistry and law)

7. *Medical Programs* (doctor of medicine, optometry, and veterinary medicine)

8. *Doctoral Degree Programs*

For each of these program categories we analyzed eight elements of cost: faculty salaries, faculty support, instructional support, library support, student services, general expense, plant operation, and administration. As a composite of all expenditures for instruction and general operation, as of 1970–71, we found this distribution:

Faculty Salaries	48%
Faculty Support	17
Instructional Service	3
Libraries	4
Student services	4
General expense	5
Plant operation	14
Administration	5
	100%

Just recently, in a staff paper accompanying the final report of the National Commission on the Financing of Postsecondary Education, a different classification of programs has been proposed. It seems to me that this classification structure is a useful one and should be generally utilized now by state governments.

In developing our models, the controlling factors were the number of faculty positions (or the student-faculty ratio) and the average compensation fixed for these positions. All other cost factors could then be determined as an historical relationship to these costs, which as I have pointed out were on the average about 48 percent of the instructional budget.

I can illustrate our practice by setting forth certain calculations employed by the Board of Regents in the 1971–73 biennium.

I wish to emphasize several aspects of this budget procedure within the Board of Regents. First of all, the model expenditure budgets were based upon institutional experi-

Politics and Higher Education

Program Categories	Student-Faculty Ratio	Average Compensation	Total Expenditure Per Student	State Subsidy Per Student
General Studies	24–1	$12,200	$1,170	$ 480
Technical Education	16–1	$12,200	$1,500	$ 810
Baccalaureate General	16–1	$15,500	$1,725	$1,035
Baccalaureate Professional	12–1	$15,500	$2,220	$1,530
Master's	10–1	$19,000	$3,090	$1,890
Graduate Professional	10–1	$19,000	$3,090	$1,890
Doctor's	8–1	$24,000	$5,190	$3,990
Medicine	6–1	$24,000	$6,600	$5,400

ence reported by the institutions themselves. Furthermore, incremental increases in the models every year or every two years were based upon requests presented by the institutions. Secondly, the models produced a *total* instructional expenditure per student by program categories. The distribution of cost between state subsidy and charges to students was a political decision to be made during the appropriation process. Thirdly, the Board of Regents calculated a total subsidy entitlement for each institution based upon estimated enrollment multiplied by that portion of the expenditure model determined to be met from state tax resources. Each university and two-year campus received a single lump sum appropriation as a subsidy. Finally, the Board of Regents did not prescribe the utilization of the subsidy by any state university or other institution. The actual distribution of the subsidy to programs and activities within a state university was an internal management decision.

The appropriation procedure in Ohio in my judgment met the two principal objectives set for it: it calculated a minimum necessary level of expenditure, and it permitted an equitable distribution of the total state appropriation among institutions according to the number of students in the major program categories. I do not claim that there were no weaknesses in this procedure. The formula was an enrollment-driven formula, and probably needs revision now that enrollment growth is declining. There were various complexities in making the necessary calculations. And on occasion the Governor and the General Assembly would question the assumptions and the data in the models. I am still convinced that the general procedure was a useful and desirable administrative practice.

Of course, there were exceptions to this formula approach. It was not workable for programs such as those of a teaching hospital, the agricultural experiment station, or the agricultural extension service. It was not workable for a small institution or a small program lacking a viable "critical mass" of student enrollment. And because Ohio law specified a special kind of tuition reduction for students enrolling at Central State University, an offsetting appropriation was needed to compensate for this reduction. No formula can or should be an avenue of escape whereby an administrator avoids exercising judgment. The need for some kind of objective equity is still an essential requirement in state government appropriations for multiple institutions of higher education, and by recent count there are nearly 900 state colleges and universities in the fifty states.

Capital Improvement Appropriations

I have discussed earlier the problem of capital improvement appropriations for state higher education. I mentioned that in November, 1963, the voters of Ohio approved a constitutional amendment that authorized a state bond issue of 250 million dollars, of which 175 million dollars were earmarked for institutions of higher education. In December, 1964, Governor Rhodes recommended a second bond issue, which was then officially submitted by the General Assembly and approved by the voters in May of 1965. This time the amount of indebtedness authorized came to 290 million dollars, of which higher education was to receive one-half. Thus in 1963 and in 1965 higher education acquired state capital improvement funds totaling 320 million dollars.

In 1967 Governor Rhodes proposed still a third bond issue, this time somewhat more complicated, calling for the creation of an Ohio Bond Commission to determine capital improvement needs and to arrange for the sale of bonds. This constitutional amendment was disapproved by the voters at the primary election of May, 1967. At that time the Board of Regents had developed a capital improvement plan calling for the expenditure of 425 million dollars between 1967 and 1975. In 1968 Governor Rhodes submitted a modified version of his 1967 plan. I had a hand in the development of this plan and considered it a major step forward in the financing of capital improvements. Fortunately, this constitutional amendment was approved by the voters at the general election of November, 1968.

Under the 1968 constitutional amendment it became possible for certain state agencies, including the state-assisted institutions of higher education, to pledge revenues derived from nonappropriated funds for the debt service of capital improvement bonds issued by a state public facility commission. All facilities to be constructed in this way had to be authorized by the General Assembly. In addition, the General Assembly had the constitutional authority to reimburse the state agencies for the revenues thus pledged for debt service. No doubt this method may seem a complex way of meeting the constitutional prohibition against a state debt, but the procedure had two immense advantages.

The first advantage was that the 1968 constitutional amendment eliminated the need for further proposals to the voters for the approval of specific bond issues. In effect, Ohio eliminated the popular referendum on the capital improvement needs of various state agencies, including the state-assisted colleges and universities. I was very grateful that we did not have to have a popular referendum in Ohio on higher education in 1969 or in 1970. The second advantage was that the General Assembly could now in effect authorize such capital improvements as it saw fit to approve and could then appropriate from the general revenue fund the amount needed to meet the debt service requirements for these capital improvements. There are many details of the arrangement which I do not need to review here. Suffice it to say that in 1968 in Ohio we finally acquired a mechanism whereby the General Assembly as representatives of the voters, rather than the voters themselves, would determine capital improvement needs and could appropriate a debt service item to defray the cost of these improvements.

Apart from the contribution of the Board of Regents to the development of this 1968 capital plant financing plan—and I consider this contribution a major accomplishment of the Board in the years between 1964 and 1972—the Board of Regents had a further task. This task was to prepare a six-year capital improvement plan of higher education needs every two years and to present this plan to the Governor and the General Assembly for their consideration. In 1968 the Congress of the United States amended the Higher Education Facilities Act of 1963 to provide some funds to each state government for facilities planning. In Ohio this money was received by the Board of

Regents and the assistance was most helpful in advancing our capacity for facilities planning.

The essentials of capital plant planning and financing embody several factors. The first is an appropriate classification of the kinds of space needed and utilized by institutions of higher education. The second step is a full inventory of existing space resources, with an evaluation of the quality of the available space: good, in need of rehabilitation, and in need of replacement. The third step was to obtain information about space utilization, and the fourth step was to establish standards of space need based upon enrollment and space utilization objectives. When the space inventory was then compared against the calculation of space needs, the net deficit became the objective for the various capital plans. Appropriations were requested to meet the deficit, to replace obsolete space, and to rehabilitate unsatisfactory space.

Here, again, the Board of Regents made use of a formula approach as a means of dividing up the available funds for capital improvements. To be sure, again no formula could meet the needs for health science center space or certain specialized space such as that for agricultural research. And the space standards were necessarily different for a two-year campus, for technical education, for a comprehensive university, and for a leading research university.

The capital improvement appropriations were never sufficient to meet all calculated needs. But continued progress was possible after 1963 in meeting the most urgent facility needs as determined by each institution. The Board of Regents undertook to calculate needs in general terms. Each institution established its own priorities in terms of specific needs. The Board of Regents did not try to exercise this judgment, and I think it should not have tried to do so. The Board might ask questions, but each institution was expected to make its own decision about priorities among specific projects and to justify that decision to those who might question it.

The Appropriation Record

I would conclude this account of financial planning in the years from 1964 to 1972 with a look at the appropriation record. We might begin with the capital improvement record. In Table 3, herewith, I summarize the capital improvement appropriations from 1963 through 1973. By way of contrast, I might mention that the total capital improvement appropriations for higher education between 1951 through 1961 came to 92 million dollars. From 1963 through 1971, the General Assembly appropriated nearly 770 million dollars for capital improvements. With the addition of federal and local funds made available between 1964 and 1972, the total amount thus invested in instructional and research facilities approached one billion dollars.

In Table 4 I have summarized the experience in appropriations for current operating purposes from 1963 through the legislative session of 1971. In this table, I have shown several categories of appropriation support and some of these call for additional comment.

The supplementary subsidies represented the developmental appropriations to Cleveland State University and Wright State University, the additional assistance provided to Central State University, the current operating appropriations for the Medical College of Ohio at Toledo, and the subsidies to the medical school of Case Western Reserve University. A one-time appropriation was also made in 1971 as start-up costs for the Ohio College Library Center, a consortium of both public and private colleges and universities for common cataloguing and book exchange service.

The research appropriation was primarily that for the agricultural experiment station, which was legally designated the Ohio Agricultural Research and Development Center. For a time the Board of Regents was also given an appropriation to support Regents Professorships at various state universities, but this appropriation was dropped in

TABLE 3
CAPITAL IMPROVEMENT APPROPRIATIONS
STATE OF OHIO
1963 THROUGH 1973

	Universities	Branches	Community Colleges	Technical Colleges	Other Agencies	Total
1963–65 S.B. 370	$ 79,633,900	$ 7,023,350	$ 2,000,000	—	$ 2,864,046	$ 91,521,296
1965–67 H.B. 204 H.B. 949	$164,620,466	$26,644,277	$10,547,000	$ 2,238,664	$11,059,286	$215,109,693
1967–69 H.B. 886	$ 2,569,088	$ 2,216,806	$ 3,303,000	$ 4,761,336	—	$ 12,850,230
1969–71 H.B. 531	$185,294,596	$25,010,000	$13,540,000	$32,075,000	$29,535,800	$286,055,396
1971–73 S.B. 4711	$ 78,483,722	$25,140,000	$19,830,000	$21,475,000	$15,050,000	$163,978,722
TOTAL	$510,601,772	$86,034,433	$49,220,000	$60,550,000	$58,509,132	$769,515,337

TABLE 4

APPROPRIATIONS OF STATE FUNDS
FOR CURRENT OPERATING PURPOSES

STATE OF OHIO

1963 THROUGH 1973

	Student Instruction	Supplementary Subsidies	Research	Public Service	Student Assistance	Overhead	Total
1963–64	$ 52,511,390	$ —	$2,163,200	$ 5,675,150	$ —	$ 100,000	$ 60,449,740
1964–65	59,681,450	—	2,163,200	5,675,150	—	150,000	67,669,800
1965–66	73,886,150	800,000	3,018,000	7,006,000	—	153,150	84,863,300
1966–67	81,767,785	960,295	3,068,000	7,371,000	—	183,250	93,100,330
1967–68	130,866,305	3,521,425	5,637,226	8,300,000	—	272,043	148,596,999
1968–69	158,393,100	3,703,250	5,640,000	8,629,781	—	355,500	176,721,631
1969–70	189,792,744	13,985,350	4,558,000	11,849,723	90,000	22,443,709	242,719,526
1970–71	202,473,147	14,450,000	4,826,000	14,345,340	4,785,103	20,377,900	261,257,490
1971–72	234,498,750	10,635,000	5,400,000	19,450,000	15,160,000	8,545,500	293,689,250
1972–73	252,067,650	9,455,000	5,600,000	20,460,000	16,160,000	21,325,000	325,067,650

1969 as research activity on campus encountered vigorous student criticism.

The appropriation for public service underwent considerable expansion during these years. Originally, as of 1963, this category included support of the agricultural extension service and the subsidy to the teaching hospitals of Ohio State. Later subsidies to teaching hospitals in Cincinnati and Toledo had to be added. Beginning in 1971 an operating appropriation was provided for the Ohio Educational Television Network and for public broadcasting by the state universities. In addition, beginning in 1969, the Board of Regents obtained appropriations to support development education for the growing number of students enrolled with distinct educational deficiencies in their preparation for undergraduate study. In 1971 subsidies to local governments where state universities were located were added.

The appropriation for student assistance was the amount provided for the Ohio Instructional Grant Program administered by the Board of Regents.

Finally, the so-called "overhead" appropriation included the operating expenses of the Ohio Board of Regents and, beginning in 1969, the debt service needed to finance the capital improvement program for the state-assisted institutions.

This record will have to speak for itself. I will say only that it was acquired with a good deal of blood, sweat, and a few impolite words thrown in on various occasions.

5

Higher Education and Politics:
Retrospect and Prospect

THERE ARE MANY GENERALIZATIONS WHICH ANY ADMINIS-
trator is tempted to draw from his experience. The biggest
temptation is of course the inclination to believe that his
decisions were always correct and that the criticisms of his
adversaries were always wrong. If at all possible, I should
like to avoid this particular temptation. Yet I recognize that
no one can ever be objective in describing his own role or in
evaluating his own performance. Nonetheless, there are
certain experiences and observations of mine that I think
well illustrate the relationship of state higher education to
state government, the relationship between higher education and politics.

Politics

Necessarily I must begin with an attempt to define the
meaning of politics as applied to the activities of state-
assisted colleges and universities. For me the term "politics"
is a word of noble purpose and great promise. Politics is the
process by which a society seeks to pursue its primary governmental goals and distributes the benefit of governmental action. It has been said that politics is the process in a
society of deciding who obtains what where and how. But
the process cannot be separated from purpose, or from the

operative ideals that establish the standards of acceptable political behavior. We cannot have a political society without politics, and long ago Aristotle observed for all of us that man is by nature a political animal.

In Ohio, as in most states of the United States, the state constitution pledged the state only to promote education for its citizens. It was left for the legislative process to determine what kinds of institutions of higher education should be established where, how they should be operated, and what resources they should be provided with in order to pursue their stated missions. Higher education conducted under state law with the assistance of state-appropriated funds is higher education engaged in politics.

Apart from the appropriation process itself—and I can think of no part of the political process that is any more political than the procedure for the appropriation of funds for various governmental services—I can illustrate the close relationship between higher education and politics by referring to the subject of access to higher education. When I went to Miami University in 1953, I discovered that there was a provision in the Ohio General Code that, in effect, guaranteed to every Ohio high school graduate admission to state-assisted higher education. This provision of law specified that no state-assisted college or university should require a test as a condition of admission to enrollment for a high school graduate. I made some inquiries in an effort to learn something about the legislative history of this law, and eventually a retired professor of education at Ohio State told me that the law was enacted in 1913 at the insistence of school administrators in Ohio who feared that college entrance examinations would come to dominate the high school curriculum. The way to preserve the independence of high school education from domination by entrance tests for admission to college was simply to forbid such tests. And this prohibition is what Ohio had done by law. This law is a perfect example of politics having its impact upon higher education.

As president of Miami University I learned that there were means of evading the requirements of the 1913 legislation. At first the university imposed no restrictions upon admission but utilized test scores as a counseling device. Applicants who scored low in academic aptitude were enrolled "on warning." This action served to discourage some applicants for admission from ever presenting themselves for actual enrollment. When applications began to exceed our housing capacity—and all freshmen except commuters were required to live in residential halls at least for the first year—we found that we could defer admission of students of poor academic quality from September to February. Again this kind of action discouraged many persons from ever enrolling at all.

Finally, it occurred to me that the enrollment of persons of poor academic aptitude was jeopardizing the financing of our housing facilities. If a student of marginal or less than average academic ability was admitted, that student was especially likely to drop out at the end of six weeks or at the end of one semester. Such a dropout reduced our room and board income, a reduction which we could not afford. And so, with the approval of the board of trustees, we began to assign housing facilities at Miami University upon the basis of academic aptitude. Of course, we continued to admit any commuting student without reference to test scores. And we found that we could interpret the provisions of the law as applying to high school graduates at the time of graduation; we did not have to admit a student who had enrolled elsewhere and then wished to enroll at Miami except in accordance with our own standards of an acceptable transfer student.

There was a time when I wondered seriously about the possibility of urging a Governor and a General Assembly to undertake to repeal the 1913 law. My inquiries on this score led me to conclude that any bill to repeal this section of the Ohio Revised Code would never emerge from a legislative committee, much less ever obtain a favorable vote on the floor of either house of the legislature. But continued experience led me to the further conclusion that open admission was a desirable social policy. Accordingly, as chancellor for the Ohio Board of Regents I worked diligently to ensure that there would be an opportunity somewhere in the system for every Ohio high school graduate who sought entry into state-assisted higher education. This objective became the first purpose of higher education planning by the Board of Regents.

State universities like to believe that they are removed from the political arena. And to a considerable extent I think they are. State universities expect boards of trustees rather than legislatures to make final decisions about many issues of higher education purpose and process: the instructional programs to offer, degree requirements, instructional procedures, student evaluation procedures, standards of student conduct, the appointment and remuneration of faculty and principal administrative officers, and similar issues. Even in the realm of support services such as purchasing, campus planning, institutional budgeting, civil service management, and campus security the state universities enjoyed a considerable range of discretion. In Ohio the state universities were required to use state civil service laws and procedures in the appointment of nonacademic personnel, to utilize the services of the state department of public works in the construction of buildings, and to depend upon the state attorney general for legal service.

The great virtue of a board of trustees for a state university is its role as surrogate for the legislative authority of the Governor and General Assembly. In higher education we expect the board of trustees rather than the legislature to enact the major laws governing the purpose and process of the enterprise. I think this arrangement is a remarkable and highly desirable practice.

And yet the authority of a board of trustees is always exercised subject to the possibility of legislative intervention. Perhaps this possibility of intervention is somewhat restricted in those states where one or more state universities have been specified in the state constitution rather than established by law. In Ohio, where all the institutions of higher education were established by law, the law could be changed or amended at any time. Whether we liked it or not, I considered higher education in Ohio at all times to be heavily involved in the political process. Unfortunately, students and faculty members often did not share this understanding of the relationship between state higher education and politics.

I also considered the Board of Regents and the position of chancellor as a further protection of the state universities in this political process. The Board of Regents became the highly visible agency of higher education in the political arena of state government. There were some university presidents who did not care for this situation. They preferred to exercise their own political influence to the fullest extent possible. It seemed to me that this position was short-sighted. The more the Ohio Board of Regents occupied the political spotlight, the more removed the state university could become from political interference. I could never quite understand why some officials of the state universities were not satisfied to escape as far as possible from the political scene. I suppose each state university president always had in the back of his mind that somehow the time and the occasion would arise when his particular institution could obtain a political advantage over some other state university, or over all other state universities.

The Political Role of the Board of Regents

This then is an appropriate place to explain in somewhat greater detail my conception of the political role of a state board of higher education and of its chief executive officer. It seems clear to me that the Ohio Board of Regents and I as chancellor were at all times highly involved in the political process of state government. The business of the Board of Regents was politics.

When I make this assertion, I do not intend to imply that the Board was or should be involved in partisan politics in a narrow sense of seeking political office or personal political advantage. I was never interested in running for elective office; in that sense I was no threat to any political officer. And there was no personal political gain which the Board of Regents was seeking for itself. I liked to explain to those who would listen that the politics of the Board of Regents was the politics of higher education.

As a state board of higher education, however, the Board of Regents was caught in an extremely difficult position. That position was halfway between the state universities on the one hand and the Governor and General Assembly on the other hand. From the point of view of the state university presidents, the political role of the Board of Regents was simple and direct: to represent the desires and aspirations of the state universities as formulated by the state universities and to persuade the political arm of state government to fulfill all of those desires. Unless the Board of Regents accepted this understanding of its role, the Board of Regents from the standpoint of the state universities was a nuisance and an unnecessary piece of governmental machinery.

From the point of view of the Governor and the General Assembly, the role of the Board of Regents was to keep the state universities in their place, to cool their aspirations, to curtail their appropriation requests, to supervise their operations, and to bring accountability into the realm of their activities. To the political arms of state government, the Board of Regents was more than a neutral or objective source of advice and counsel about the needs of public higher education. The Board of Regents was expected to assist the Governor and General Assembly in the enactment and the supervision of desirable state policies that represented a state-wide interest rather than the interest of any one institution.

As I saw the role of the Board of Regents, it was to assist state government in finding and expressing the politically desirable and feasible policies concerning higher education, which simultaneously achieved a socially responsible higher education endeavor and a maximum degree of institutional autonomy. I always tried to draw a reasonable line of distinction between state government policy-making in higher education and institutional management. The Board of Regents had a role to play, an important role I thought, in the realm of state higher education policy. The Board of Regents had no role to play in the internal management affairs of any particular state university.

This distinction between policy and management in higher education is not simple to draw or to observe in practice. I am well aware of the point of view of those who argue that the distinction cannot be drawn in logic or in observance. While I readily acknowledge that policy and management are closely interrelated, I also insisted that a distinction should be attempted and could be realized. If this distinction cannot be made, then there is no future for state boards of higher education but only a future for one or more state governing boards of higher education.

Policy and Management

I can best discuss this distinction between policy and management by means of a number of examples drawn from our experience in Ohio. I hope these examples will demonstrate how the distinction was observed in the years from 1964 to 1972 when I was endeavoring to define it.

Let me begin by mentioning several successful efforts by the Board of Regents to strengthen and preserve the management autonomy of the state universities. I always considered House Bill No. 307 of the 106th General Assembly a major achievement. This legislation, approved by Governor Rhodes on June 15, 1965, effective September 15, 1965, amended two sections of the Revised Code pertaining to state financial management and the authority of state university boards of trustees. The essence of the new law was that state universities henceforth were not required to deposit student instructional charges with the Treasurer of State but could retain these collections in their own accounts. Previously, the state universities had to deposit all student instructional and general fees in the state treasury and these were then reappropriated to the respective universities in the same amounts as collected. Room and board charges were not handled in this way, however. The new law was part of my effort to have the state universities considered as state government corporations receiving a state subsidy for their operation.

I used several arguments for this change. If the universities were competent to handle room and board charges, they were competent to handle instructional charges. If the State paid a single subsidy amount to the state universities, a great deal of paper work and considerable administrative costs in Columbus could be eliminated. If school districts handled their own funds, including state subsidies, so could the state universities. And with state universities about to undergo a great enrollment expansion, it would be desirable to decentralize this administrative burden. Now in my judgment all of these were and are good, sound arguments. But they would never have carried the day by themselves.

As work proceeded on the Governor's budget to go to the General Assembly in January, 1965, I knew Governor Rhodes was concerned about the size of the appropriation increases to be requested for the 1965–67 biennium over the 1963–65 biennium. In 1966 Governor Rhodes would stand for reelection. It seemed to me that the time was appropriate for a change in the state budget and appropriation procedure affecting the state universities. One day in conversation with Governor Rhodes, I told him I knew how he could eliminate 20 million dollars from the executive budget without any trouble. He was at once interested. I reminded him how the news media simply reported budget totals of one biennium compared with the previous biennium, and that details of income and expense seldom received any public attention. Therefore, I proposed that the reappropriation of student fees be eliminated from the executive budget and that the state universities be permitted by law to retain control over these collections. The amounts involved would then automatically disappear from the executive budget. Governor Rhodes liked the idea and requested me to pursue the matter further with the Director of Finance. The Director of Finance approved my proposal, endorsed the legislation we prepared, and pushed its enactment on behalf of the Governor. And thereby the Board of Regents won a major victory for the management autonomy of the state universities.

Similarly, as issues arose in 1968 and in 1970 about the maintenance of law and order on university campuses, I insisted that this responsibility rested with the individual boards of trustees and generally succeeded in having the two laws enacted in those years to reflect this principle. In 1967 with the assistance of the Director of Finance, I was able to persuade two legislative committees to give the state universities greater authority in handling the recruitment and appointment of civil service personnel, subject to audit by the department of state personnel. This new authority was threatened in 1969 and again by a new and ambitious Director of State Personnel under Governor Gilligan in 1971. With some small compromises, the principle of decentralization of personnel matters was maintained. There were also several assaults upon the law that permitted the state universities to do their own purchasing, but I defended this practice as vigorously as I could and the law was not changed while I was chancellor.

An important part of the political role of the Ohio Board of Regents was to prevent legislation as much as to seek legislation. In every session of the General Assembly a number of bills would be introduced to determine how certain aspects of state university operations were to be handled. These bills might restrict printing contracts to Ohio printers, or give free tuition to school teachers, or direct the opening of some new program in a particular place. These bills might restrict faculty and student activity, or require all purchasing to be done through the state division of purchases. I continually had to exert such influence as I could to prevent the favorable consideration of these and similar measures.

It came as a surprise to me to discover that when a group of faculty members are dissatisfied with a situation, they are not above seeking political intervention, on their side of course. I thought the principle of no political intervention was widely understood and supported. I was wrong. For example, the President and Board of Trustees at Ohio State decided to eliminate the laboratory school where a number of faculty children were enrolled. The President and his advisers decided that this laboratory school served no useful purpose for the teacher education program. The faculty parents first wanted me and then wanted the General Assembly to reverse this decision. The desired action was blocked, but I was amazed by the lack of principle involved in the requested intervention.

I always argued that the Board of Regents had no role in matters of curriculum and degree requirements, no role in faculty affairs including faculty compensation, and no role in student affairs. Some of the student affairs officers thought I was demonstrating a hostile point of view toward their activities. On the contrary, from my experience as a state university president, I had nothing but the highest regard for the student affairs personnel on our various state university campuses. I was insistent only that the

Board of Regents had no authority to intervene in any of these matters.

When student disruptions began in 1968 in Ohio, continued in 1969, and culminated in the tragedy of May 4, 1970, at Kent State University, the boards of trustees and the presidents of the individual state universities had the authority and the responsibility to handle these situations. The Board of Regents had no authority of government to intervene if we had wanted to, and I did not want to. In September, 1969, I had taken Governor Rhodes to Cleveland to spend a day visiting the new facilities of Cleveland State University, of Cuyahoga Community College, and of Case Western Reserve medical center (which the state had not built but was now helping to support). At a news conference in Cleveland that day, the Governor announced his intention to assist boards of trustees to maintain law and order on state university campuses, even if it meant using the national guard. Governor Rhodes did not consult me before he made this statement, and in private conversation afterwards I told him I thought his position was wrong. He defended it on the grounds that the voters of Ohio were upset about campus disruption.

Although I had only bits and pieces of gossip picked up inside state government as the basis for my opinion, I suspected that campus disruption was not entirely a matter of local leadership. It appeared that there were some outside instigators who came to our state university campuses and then quickly went away again. In fact, I had been told that Kent State University was a major target of outside interest in 1969. But my position with the Governor was that repression or overreaction to these actions was exactly what the plotters wanted, if there were such plotters. I also thought that the presidents should handle these situations according to their own assessment of the circumstances, and that outside forces should be used only when requested by boards of trustees.

I also found that the presidents had great respect for the Ohio State Highway Patrol, whose men were well trained and highly disciplined, while the presidents were inclined to be much less enthusiastic about national guard units, which seemed to be less well trained and less well disciplined. This assessment of relative capabilities seemed to be borne out on May 4, 1970.

After the Kent State tragedy occurred, my only role was to protect the University from political reprisal. There were mutterings about various kinds of legislation, and a tough law and order bill, House Bill No. 1219, was passed on June 5, 1970, approved by the Governor on June 17, and became law on September 16, 1970. My associate, James Furman, worked valiantly to obtain substantial modification of this bill in the Senate and succeeded in doing so. It was a very difficult period of time. Never was the importance of having political friends more clearly demonstrated than during these weeks.

One other item might be mentioned. When the taxation-appropriation measure was before the General Assembly in 1967, the then Director of Finance, Richard Krabach, remarked to me one day that there were many legislators and public opinion leaders who had considerable reservations about management competence within the state universities. Although I did not share this view, I acquiesced in his proposal that, as a desirable political action, the state should undertake a major study of management practices in state higher education. As a result, a management consulting firm in Chicago was retained by the Department of Finance in conjunction with an education review committee set up by the General Assembly.

The report of this management survey was submitted to the education review committee late in 1969. In general, the findings contained few surprises. The consultants did recommend that the Board of Regents should take a more active part in university management by supervising various activities such as the use of computers, the handling of supply purchases, and the performance of budgeting and accounting. I was opposed to these recommendations because they did not correspond with my philosophy of the desirable relationship between the Board of Regents and the state universities.

There was considerable discussion among legislative leaders about the action they should take to follow up this management study. I was able finally to assist the leaders in arriving at a solution. I certainly didn't want a bill enacted that had been introduced to carry out every single recommendation of the consultants. I suggested that the whole matter be referred to the Legislative Service Commission and that the Commission retain an impartial adviser to work out a compromise. And then even more informally I suggested that the Commission ask Mr. C. W. Ingler, director of community relations for the National Cash Register Company, to serve as its adviser. Both suggestions were adopted.

I had great confidence in Mr. Ingler, whom I had known since his service as director of the Legislative Service Commission. He had been first chairman of the Interim Commission on Education Beyond the High School back in 1959 and 1960. Moreover, in his role at National Cash Register, Mr. Ingler had helped greatly in bringing about the creation of Wright State University and the Montgomery County community college. I was sure Mr. Ingler would be equally fair to both the Board of Regents and the state universities. Nor was I disappointed in my expectation. Mr. Ingler worked out a plan whereby the Board of Regents and the state universities would jointly undertake a management improvement program. The product of this program was to be a series of management manuals of best practice for the guidance of the state universities. The

Board of Regents was to take the leadership in the development of these manuals but was not to assume any role in supervising their implementation.

I thought Mr. Ingler's proposals were quite helpful in the circumstances. The Republican leadership in the General Assembly decided to embody the Ingler compromise in the appropriation legislation of 1971, and Governor Gilligan went along with the recommendation. The appropriation law finally enacted on December 20, 1971, authorized a management improvement program under the leadership of the Board of Regents. The program got under way in 1972 and some ten manuals (five for the state universities and five for the two-year campuses) were completed in 1974. I had hoped to persuade Mr. Ingler to come to the Board of Regents as vice-chancellor to direct this program, but several months before our appropriation law in Ohio was enacted, Chancellor Boyer of the State University of New York invited Mr. Ingler to join his staff in Albany, which he did.

I think I have reviewed these various incidents or episodes in sufficient detail to make clear my attempted distinction between the policy role of the Board of Regents in the state capital and the management role of the various state universities on their respective campuses. I still believe the proper role of a state board of higher education is advice on state policy, and that a state university board of trustees must assume management authority and responsibility. But I must acknowledge that many political leaders wanted to see more and more authority of governance and management over the state universities centralized in Columbus. These leaders were unhappy about the increasing demands of faculty and students for a role in university governance and they lacked confidence in boards of trustees and presidents to enforce rigorous management procedures. Moreover, the decentralization of management outside of Columbus prevented political leaders from maintaining close watch over management actions. It remained to be seen whether or not the 1971 compromise on management of the universities would be mutually satisfactory to the state universities and to the political leadership of the State of Ohio.

Political Power and Influence in Higher Education

When I went to Columbus from Miami University in 1964, I asked myself from time to time what power or influence higher education had in the political process of state government. My first inclination was to look for an effective interest group that might be helpful in presenting a higher education point of view to the Governor and the General Assembly. I quickly learned that there was no such interest group. The Ohio Farm Bureau Federation was interested in support of the College of Agriculture, the Agricultural Research and Development Center, and the agricultural extension service. I soon developed friendly relations with the Farm Bureau and found its assistance helpful on occasion.

Both the State Chamber of Commerce and the Ohio Manufacturers Association were disposed to be supportive of Governor Rhodes and on occasion to be supportive of my efforts on behalf of higher education, but this interest was neither intense nor continuing. The various professional associations such as the Ohio Medical Association, the Ohio Bar Association, the Ohio Dental Association, and the Ohio League of Nursing were quite interested in professional welfare, including professional education. But I was never aware of any assistance which I could expect or rely upon coming from these groups.

It was very apparent to me that the situation in higher education was quite different from that in elementary-secondary education. On the one hand, the state administrative agency in elementary-secondary education was the

State Board of Education whose members were elected by the voters in the state's congressional districts; the State Superintendent of Public Instruction was then appointed by this board. On the other hand, there was the Ohio Education Association composed of some 90,000 of the 110,000 public school teachers of Ohio. The elected board of directors of the OEA appointed an executive director and a legislative representative. I learned quickly that the OEA was one of the most powerful lobbying organizations in Columbus. Moreover, it was wonderful to behold how loyal and supportive all 90,000 teachers throughout Ohio were to the Ohio Education Association.

In fact, my one major political defeat suffered in my eight years in Columbus was administered by the Ohio Education Association. I had advocated and I had obtained the endorsement of Governor Rhodes for legislation that would permit faculty members in the state universities to elect the privately operated Teachers Insurance and Annuity Association of New York as an alternative to the State Teachers Retirement System, which was dominated by the public school system in Ohio. I discovered that I had raised a whole raft of issues involving social security, state regulation of the insurance industry, private profit-making insurance versus private nonprofit-making insurance, and of course the bureaucratic self-interest of the State Teachers Retirement System. But the coup de grace was administered by the Ohio Education Association behind the scenes. The OEA was opposed to letting university faculty members out of the state teachers retirement program, and this opposition was a matter of economics. Most public school teachers were women, and most university faculty members were men. If these men had been removed from the actuarial calculations of the teachers retirement fund, the contributions of both the teachers and the school districts would have had to be increased. The OEA wasn't about to let this increase happen. My proposed bill was buried in committee.

The OEA representatives later vigorously denied that they had brought any pressure to bear to defeat my proposal. They claimed that the private profit-making insurance industry and the administrators of the retirement system killed the legislation. I never believed these disclaimers. Insofar as I was concerned, whenever there was a conflict of interest between higher education and school education, the OEA was to be found on the side of school education.

By way of contrast, there was absolutely no counterpart to OEA in the higher education world of Ohio. As of 1972 there were about 36,000 full-time positions in the state universities and in the two-year campuses. About 22,000 of these positions were made up of instructional staff. There were about 2,500 professional staff, including principal administrators, and the remaining 11,500 positions were made up of clerical, fiscal, housekeeping, maintenance, and crafts positions. There was almost no sense of cohesion or common interest among all these persons, and they were not organized in any way to exercise any influence upon the political process in Columbus.

Both the Ohio Civil Service Employees Association and the American Federation of State, County, and Municipal Employees tried to organize the maintenance, housekeeping, and other nonprofessional personnel of the state universities, and by 1972 had won a sizeable membership. These two groups were interested exclusively in civil service rates of pay and certain working conditions; I never sensed that they had any particular interest in higher education as such. The Ohio Education Association tried to recruit members from higher education faculties, but with indifferent success. I hoped faculty members perceived that there was a conflict of interest when the OEA tried to represent

both higher education and elementary-secondary education. Some modest efforts at organizing faculties under the
auspicies of the American Association of University Profes-
sors were made in Ohio. The trouble is that faculty members are too individually minded to be effective organization members, to be an effective interest group.

And so as I looked around and as the years proceeded, I
found that there was no interest group to rely upon for
assistance on political matters affecting higher education.
And if there was an elite power structure in Ohio, I never
found it. To be sure, there was a power structure, a very
definite power structure, in the various large cities such as
Cleveland, Cincinnati, Columbus, Akron, Toledo, Dayton,
Youngstown, and Canton. Many members of these power
structures served as members of the Board of Regents and
as members of state university boards of trustees. There
were power structures in other communities. And in the
course of time, I became acquainted with many of these
persons and became good friends with some. They were
disposed to be personally supportive for the most part, but
this power elite was never a coherent, incisive group for the
exercise of political power or influence.

As I searched I could find only two instruments of political power upon whom to rely. One was the Governor. And
the second was the leadership in the General Assembly, the
leadership of both parties. If this leadership was disposed to
be friendly toward the state universities and higher education in general, then we fared well. And this disposition to
be friendly seemed to be a highly personal matter, depend-
ing upon the personal attitudes of the Governor and of
legislators and how well I was able to work with these
individuals.

For better or for worse, I found that my influence depended in large part upon my relationship to the Governor.
Governor Rhodes and I became friends; I came to like and
to respect him. I think he liked me. I did not and could not

have the same relationship to Governor Gilligan after January, 1971. Let me review some of this story.

The Special Session of 1964 and the Regular Session of 1965

My close working association with Governor Rhodes began on Tuesday, November 3, 1964. It was a general election day, and the Governor called me to his office in the morning. He told me that he was certain the election would be a disaster for the Republican party. He was partly right. Lyndon Johnson carried the Ohio presidential election by a plurality over Barry Goldwater of one million votes. The Republican party barely maintained control of the Ohio House of Representatives and the Ohio Senate in 1965 was evenly divided between sixteen Republicans and sixteen Democrats. In anticipation of some such result, the Governor informed me that he planned to call the 1963 General Assembly into special session in December in order to enact several pieces of legislation before the 1965 General Assembly would come into office. He told me that he would include higher education matters in his call and asked me what I was prepared to recommend to him and the special session. I requested and was given twenty-four hours in which to respond.

The next twenty-four hours were hectic indeed. The Board of Regents was in the process of preparing its first Master Plan but the full range of our proposals was not yet agreed upon. I telephoned the Board members and got immediate agreement upon two matters: the creation of a state university in Cleveland and the establishment of a new medical college in Toledo. To these Governor Rhodes added a new capital bond issue to be submitted to the voters for approval in May, 1965. My staff worked with the staff of the Legislative Service Commission in drafting the necessary bills, and House Bill No. 2 and House Bill No. 7 of the

Special Session were matters of law before Christmas of 1964. The Board of Regents was under way in its planning.

The 1965 General Assembly was not a period of inaction, however, insofar as higher education was concerned. The Universities of both Akron and Toledo had reached the point in their development where they were prepared to become state-sponsored rather than municipally sponsored institutions. Actually, some interest in a shift of status had been evident for several years. I insisted with my board members that the initiative for a change in status should originate with the two universities and not with our Board. At the same time I discussed the matter with Governor Rhodes and found him receptive to the change. As a consequence, Senate Bill No. 212 of the 106th Ohio General Assembly provided for the creation of two new state universities to succeed to the operation, assets, and liabilities of the two municipal universities. This legislation was enacted by both houses and approved by the Governor on August 12, 1965. A companion piece of legislation, Senate Bill No. 210, provided for the creation of Wright State University in Dayton as successor to a university branch campus jointly operated by Miami University and Ohio State University. This measure was approved by the Governor on August 6, 1965. Thus additional major elements in the Master Plan of the Board of Regents began to take shape.

The 1967 General Assembly

In November, 1966, Governor Rhodes was reelected to serve a second term, defeating his Democratic opponent by a plurality of more than 700,000 votes. Substantial majorities for the Republican party were returned in both houses of the General Assembly. The new year of 1967 promised to be of major importance for Ohio higher education, and this expectation was realized, but not without difficulty.

As soon as the 1966 election was ended, it was clear that Governor Rhodes would have to recommend a tax increase to the new General Assembly. It was also clear that the tax increase would probably be a one percent increase in the sales tax, from 3 percent to 4 percent. The problem was how this tax increase was to be presented and made politically acceptable. As these discussions continued, I learned that the Rhodes Administration had decided upon two major items of strategy. The first was to present a balanced budget to the General Assembly within the limits of currently available tax revenues. The second was to present a second budget that would be a combined taxation and appropriation measure, increasing the sales tax and restricting the use of the additional income to the school foundation program and to higher education.

Governor Rhodes explained to me that he was determined that members of the legislature should not have an opportunity to vote on increased expenditures without at the same time having to vote for increased taxation. In this connection the Governor indicated two other considerations to me. He wanted to complete the general outlines of the higher education program in the 1967 General Assembly. This year was the time to accomplish our major objectives and to include their cost in the combined appropriation-taxation package. And secondly, he told me that he intended to give higher education the larger proportionate share of the increased appropriation. Governor Rhodes was not a favorite of the Ohio Education Association, and he felt that the OEA behind the scenes had been hostile to his campaign for reelection. While I had no part of any kind in the reelection campaign, the Governor was grateful to the Board of Regents for its discussion of higher education progress being made in Ohio.

As a result of this strategy, the Board of Regents joined with various legislators in advocating two new measures, one of which established Youngstown State University as a

successor institution to a private university in that city and
the other of which gave the University of Cincinnati a new
status as a municipally sponsored, state-related university.
Under this arrangement the State of Ohio was to begin to
provide a subsidy to the University for graduate and
graduate professional programs and for nursing. The University officials and the power structure of Cincinnati indicated their desire to retain a dual status of this kind rather
than to become completely a state university.

In terms of appropriations, the supplemental legislation,
which became law on September 1, 1967, increased the
higher education appropriation by 75 million dollars and
increased the school foundation and state department of
education appropriation by 216 million dollars. Higher
education received an increase of 33 percent above the
original appropriation, and the school foundation program
received an increase of 25 percent. Of the new revenue to
be realized from the sales tax, higher education received 25
percent and the school foundation program received 75
percent. Of the original educational appropriations higher
education had received 22 percent. Thus, higher education
gained some ground in 1967 in relation to elementary-
secondary education.

Needless to say, this relationship did not go unobserved
in the General Assembly or by the Ohio Education Association. Because the basic law establishing the school foundation program had to be revised in order to authorize larger
state appropriations, the substantive education law had to
be amended along with the taxation-appropriation measure. These amendments were scrutinized with great care
in the Senate Education Committee, where the Republican,
as well as the Democratic, members were especially inclined
to be responsive to the OEA point of view.

One hot day in August of 1967, I received word from the
Legislative Service Commission that the Senate Education
Committee had decided to increase the school foundation

formula beyond that recommended by the Governor, and so it would be necessary to reduce the supplementary appropriation to higher education by 10 million dollars. The director of the Commission simply asked me to assist him in making the necessary cuts on an equitable basis. I was not at all disposed, however, to make these reductions. I learned that the Senate Education Committee was meeting in the Senate Caucus Room behind closed doors. I went immediately to that room. The first person I encountered leaving the room was the OEA legislative representative. I told him in no uncertain terms what I thought of this raid upon the higher education appropriation. Then I encountered the State Superintendent of Instruction and paid him my compliments. To the assembled and somewhat astonished members of the Senate Education Committee, I spoke my opposition with clarity and anger.

I then went downstairs in the State Capitol to see Governor Rhodes. He saw me at once, and I reported the events in the Senate Caucus Room. The Governor asked me to calm down and then reminded me that he possessed the authority of item veto. He pledged his efforts to reverse the decision, and at once sent a message to that effect to the Capitol press room. Within twenty-four hours the Republican leadership reversed its position, and the appropriations as recommended by the Governor were enacted. My relations with the Senate leadership were somewhat strained by this episode, but my relationship to Governor Rhodes had become one of close personal alliance.

In 1967 the Ohio General Assembly decided that it would meet in short session in the even-numbered years. Early in 1968 the General Assembly considered and enacted an important part of the program of the Board of Regents, a law approved March 8, 1968, establishing a higher educational facility commission to assist private colleges and universities in borrowing money for plant improvements. This law enabled private institutions to borrow funds at interest rates comparable to those available to the public institutions. It was an essential part of our endeavor to provide state government assistance to private higher education. Since it did not cost the state any money—it did reduce federal government income tax collections from wealthy payers—the measure was favorably considered by the General Assembly.

In August, 1968, while attending a meeting in Denver, I had a telephone call from the chairman of the Republican State Committee advising me that Governor Rhodes wished me to be the speaker nominating the Governor for President at the Republican National Convention the following week in Miami Beach. I was convinced that this political role was not an appropriate one for me to assume. I called the chairman of the Board of Regents fully expecting him to veto the matter. But instead I learned that my chairman was the one in the first place who had suggested my assuming this assignment. I felt that I had no choice except to honor the request or to resign my position. Knowing something about the political aspects of the situation and realizing that there were still things I wanted to do for higher education in Ohio, I reluctantly accepted the request.

I knew that Governor Rhodes was a favorite son candidate for the Republican nomination solely to prevent a bitter conflict from developing between the Nixon supporters and the more liberal elements of the Republican Party in Ohio. I also knew that Governor Rhodes did not want to favor either faction of the Party at the Republican National Convention. I then became a "dark-horse" speaker at the Republican National Convention in 1968, a speaker whom the national news media and everyone else completely ignored. I was at least thankful for this lack of publicity. I think in professional terms my appearance at the Republican National Convention was a mistake. In political terms my appearance was not a mistake. In 1969 the Board of Regents made further gains in higher education legislation and appropriations. I never heard of any administrators or faculty members who rejected the additional funds provided in 1969.

The 1969 Appropriation

In the 1968 presidential election Richard Nixon defeated Hubert Humphrey in Ohio by just 91,000 votes. George Wallace received over 465,000 votes. Legislative control in Ohio remained in the hands of the Republicans, and once again higher education was a major subject of concern. This time the Rhodes Administration decided to present two budgets to the General Assembly, one for general governmental expenditures including public welfare and mental health and a second for education expenditures. The strategy once more was to compel the General Assembly to face the issues of appropriations and taxation to support the elementary-secondary and the higher education services of the state. The result was one appropriation bill that became law on July 2, 1969, and another approved on August 18, 1969. This time many substantive issues of law were included in the appropriation legislation. To me the most important of these was the creation of the Ohio Instructional Grant program providing direct financial assistance to Ohio youth from families below the median family income in the state. Moreover, these grants were available to high school graduates enrolling in private as well as public institutions. The grant amounts were higher for students in private institutions, thus embodying the principle of tuition equalization. The appropriation law also fixed enrollment limitations for various campuses and authorized support of the medical education program at Case Western Reserve.

I thought that the 1969 legislation achieved completion of all the original objectives of the 1965 Master Plan of the Ohio Board of Regents. Moreover, the appropriations of

504 million dollars for 1969–71 represented a 54 percent increase over the appropriation for 1967–69.

During the calendar year 1970 the Board of Regents worked upon the preparation of a new Master Plan, which was completed and published in January, 1971. In the meantime, John J. Gilligan, Democrat of Cincinnati, was elected Governor on November 3, 1970. The control of the General Assembly remained with the Republican party.

On the whole I thought Governor Gilligan was generous in his attitude toward me personally, although we had only occasional contact. His Director of Finance, however, was inclined to be quite supportive. The Governor adopted the strategy of his predecessor in combining in one piece of legislation matters of substantive law, a new tax program, and appropriations. The political maneuvering was lengthy and exhausting. The combined legislation was not enacted until December 10, 1971, and did not become law until signed by Governor Gilligan on December 20.

It was simply not to be expected that higher education would fare as well for 1971–73 as it had fared in the two previous biennia. In the 1969–71 biennium higher education received better than 16 percent of the appropriations from the general revenue fund. For 1971–73 the proportion dropped to 14 percent. The increase for higher education between the two biennia was 20 percent; the increase for the school foundation program was 45 percent. Need I add that the Ohio Education Association had endorsed the candidacy of John Gilligan in the 1970 election.

I was able to assert such influence as I could upon the 1971 appropriation process only through the Republican leadership in both houses. For the most part, the leadership group was supportive, but one of them told me candidly that higher education had had its day in the sun from 1967 to 1971. Without a strong friend in the Governor's position, higher education was not able to do so well as in earlier years. Obviously, it was time for me to retire from the political scene and let someone else develop new working relationships with the Governor and General Assembly of Ohio. And I did so in 1972.

Conclusion

As I look ahead at what lies in prospect for higher education planning in the fifty states, I am prepared to stand by two forecasts. One is that the future of higher education policy and decision-making rests upon the political relationship between the higher education community and the political leadership of a state. This expectation is the lesson of past experience, including my own experience in Ohio, and I know no reason to anticipate a change in the foreseeable future. The second forecast is that the higher education community will remain weak and divisive in its approach to the political power of state government.

As I read the record of public higher education in the United States, which means a record largely compiled in fifty different state governments, I am surprised that higher education has fared as well as it has. In large part, I think that record was made possible by three things. The first was the reservoir of public good will accumulated by the remarkable contributions of higher education to the military success of World War II, including the atomic bomb. The second influence was the Russian accomplishment in space in 1957 and the fright that this achievement occasioned for American science, American technology, and American higher education. The immediate response was to spend more money for university research and various instructional programs. The third influence was the increasing inclination of American youth to enroll in colleges and universities, an inclination encouraged and made possible by the remarkable economic growth of the United States from 1945 through 1973. Higher education had a certain amount of public popularity during these years, and in various states among various political personalities higher education had a number of friends. Many of these friends became state governors: in California, in New York, in Ohio, and elsewhere.

It is almost a cliché to observe today that higher education has lost much of its public appeal, that public interest has turned to other priorities, that our colleges and universities have lost the confidence of important segments of our society. To some extent I believe this interpretation is accurate. The reasons are many, and too complicated to summarize in any adequate way.

But for me the principal concern is still the same as it was in my Ohio years from 1953 to 1972: the relationship of higher education to the political process of state government. The political process itself is little understood or appreciated by academic personnel, including students, faculties, and administrators. But even more important than the process itself is the relationship of the higher education community to the process. And here the record is especially dismal.

Colleges and universities want to isolate themselves from the political process. They are fearful of political controls, of political interference with their learning activity and with their criticism of social performance. Moreover, these fears are not without foundation in experience.

Yet at the same time when there is this concern for isolation from the political process, there is also this yearning within the academic community for increased public funding, for higher salaries, for a lower student-faculty ratio, for more support of faculty research and public service, for better facilities and equipment, for more financial assistance to students, for lower or stabilized charges to students. All of these needs are considered to be self-evident, and only the perversity of society and of politics presumably prevents these needs from being fulfilled.

Politics is not the process of meeting felt needs; it is the process of responding to economic and social forces that compel political action. Higher education has been a compelling social force in the past. It might become a compelling social force in the future. Time will tell.

Whatever happens, however, higher education must have political spokesmen—spokesmen who understand the glory of higher education but can talk the language of practical politics, spokesmen who seek great ends while pursuing reasonable and ethical compromise. Moreover, these spokesmen must have support, not continued criticism, because they are not perfect in word or deed. I tried to be such a spokesman in one state for one brief moment in time.

There will surely be others in the years ahead who can and will bring about that mutual respect and dependence between politics and higher education upon which the future of this last great hope of Western civilization must rely in order to fulfill its commitment, its promise, and its impossible dream.

Index